OUT OF NORFOLK

The Lives of Some Norfolk Seamen and Travellers

OUT OF NORFOLK

The Lives of Some Norfolk Seamen and Travellers

PETER ELPHICK

(The title of this book has been taken from the title of the poem by William Cowper on the subject of the portrait of his mother. She was born at Ludham Hall in the County, and the poet himself died at, and is buried in, East Dereham.)

ORLANDO PUBLISHING
Chequers Cottage
Church Lane
Briston
Norfolk NR24 2LF

First Published in 1988 by
Orlando Publishing
Briston Norfolk
Printed by Witley Press Ltd
Hunstanton Norfolk

ISBN 1 870982 01 0

This book is dedicated to my wife, who has been very patient with me in my quest for Norfolk seamen and has, indeed, accompanied and aided me on many of the research field-trips involved. Perhaps her interest in things maritime was generated by the place of her birth. She was born in the end residence of the row of houses that were later pulled down so that the drydock for the *Cutty Sark* could be constructed. She was born almost exactly where the *Cutty Sark's* bowsprit is now, in its Greenwich base.

Contents

Preface

Back in 1662, a long time before most of the sailors mentioned in this book had been born, Thomas Fuller in his "Worthies of England" commented upon the nautical standing of Norfolk. He said, *"No Country in England doth carry a top and top-gallant more high in maritime performance than Norfolk."*

If this was true in the 17th century, then nothing that has happened since has in any way detracted from that statement. Nelson, Vancouver, Marryat, Keppel and Hoste, sailors of renown all, have been born in, or lived in, the county since that date. Others of equal fame and many who gained no fame at all, have all added to the maritime ambience of this particular corner of England.

Why has Norfolk produced, or played host to, so many notable seamen? The county's geographical aspect must have something to do with it. It has a long coastline with the sea on two sides. It once had several more thriving ports than the few that exist now. Blakeney, Cley, Wiveton and Salthouse, were all ports of some significance. Its fishing ports have been the training schools for many sailors, and even its land-locked Broads must have produced watermen who later went to sea.

Furthermore, Norfolk is an agricultural county, and farmers and seamen have always had much in common; (as we shall see, several of the sailors mentioned in this book ended up as farmers). Both have to battle the elements in their respective callings, and both have to possess the necessary skills to ensure that they win that battle most of the time. Both types of men are of an independent and self-reliant character.

Let us not forget the old Norfolk saying that 'A Norfolk man is born with one foot on the land, and the other in the water'. Visit any of the churches along the Norfolk coast, and the chances are that they will have a 'sailor's corner', or a 'fisherman's corner', or a board recording the rescues that the local boat was involved in. A walk around the graveyards associated with those churches will reveal numerous graves with maritime connections. Norfolk would be near the top of any county league table based on matters of marine significance.

The seamen and travellers portrayed in this book were native bred, or came to reside in the county for a time. In one or two cases, they have been included simply because they were buried here. In other words, the author has been flexible. A more rigid rule for inclusion would have meant that several of the most famous of our sailors would have had to be left out. Even Nelson would have been omitted, for after he became famous he rarely returned to the county of his birth, although he always maintained the deepest regard for it.

Almost all the seamen included in this book are men who gained high rank in one or other of the sea services of England; men from the quarterdeck in fact. There are a few exceptions, but not many. It had been the author's original intention to include more representatives from the lower deck. However, assiduous research has failed to reveal any written narrative or record made by or about any 'ordinary' seaman from Norfolk. Apparently this county has not produced a Herman Melville, or a Richard Dana, or even a James Morrison, (boatswain of the *Bounty* who kept a journal of the famous mutiny and its aftermath).

In an endeavour to make up for this lack of balance, stories about individuals from the lower deck have been included wherever it seemed relevant to do so. This approach may well have met with Nelson's approval. As he once said, *'Aft the more glory, but forward the better men'*.

The author has received information, help, and advice, from many people within the county. He would like to thank especially, Mr. N. A. Linge who first put him on the track of Captain Woodget's grandson, and Major James Forsythe for leading him to Lieut. Colonel Knights. A special thanks too, must go to Mr. Raymond Page, for allowing me to see and to use information from his admirably complete family history.

Three of the sailors mentioned in this book are still very much with us. For giving up some of their time, and for loaning me pictures and documents, the author's thanks go to Lieut. Commander Edgar Woodget, to Richard Morris, and to John Pask. Long may they stay hale and hearty.

It would be an injustice not to mention the help I have received from the staff of the Lynn Museum. The same sentiment applies to all those anonymous local historians, the authors of Church Guides throughout Norfolk. Their publications often contained clues that led to interesting discoveries.

Introduction — to set the scene

The seamen and travellers who are the subjects of the following pen portraits range in date from the 14th century to the present one. Much has changed over the intervening centuries, and yet some things have not altered. The sea has not changed, and neither have some of the seamanship skills necessary to fight that element in its dark moods. Furthermore, part of the pride that the seaman of today has in his calling is based on traditions of service which were first generated centuries ago.

Until the days of Elizabeth I, there was little to distinguish the merchant ship from the warship. When circumstances demanded it, the merchantman became the man-or-war, and when the national danger was over, it reverted to its former role. In later centuries, some merchant ships were run very much on naval lines; the best examples of this being the ships of the East India Company.

Up to Stuart times there was often little to distinguish the sailor from the soldier, especially in the officer ranks. In Commonwealth and Restoration times, when Myngs, Narborough, and Shovell flourished, most of the men who served as admirals were in fact generals. They included men like Blake, Prince Rupert, and the 1st Duke of Albemarle (General Monck). There were also plenty of 'gentlemen' commanders in the navy, men who had been given their commands as a result of patronage and favour, rather than on ability and experience. Samuel Pepys did a great deal to help abolish this practice (although 'favour' in the sense of preferment for one's followers, remained a factor in the navy almost to the present day) and certainly, 'tarpaulin' captains like the three from Norfolk already mentioned, who were professionals after a life spent at sea, were infinitely preferred by the men who served under them. Sailors were no fools, and if they were going to risk their lives, they preferred to do it under someone who knew his business.

Terms and conditions of employment for seamen changed dramatically over the period covered by these pen portraits, of course. We can say that life at sea up to the 18th century was harsh, then it got better and became just hard. Even nowadays, it is no life for the weak and soft.

Until well into this century, life on board ship was hard for all, but it was especially so for the lower deck seamen. To generalize, we can say that accommodation, food, and hygiene arrangements, were of the poorest order up to the beginning of the 18th century. Things then began to improve, but even in the early 19th century ships were still often infested with rats, lice and fleas. In bad weather when the 'heads' near the bow could not be used, bilges were used as latrines, and the stench below decks was awful.

Overcrowding was always a problem on naval ships. Their complements had to be high enough to fight the ship as well as to work it, and high enough too to make up for the expected losses from battles and disease during the course of the voyage. Merchant ships were not overcrowded. Here, numbers were kept to the minimum necessary to work the ship, and in consequence the merchant seaman had to work very much harder than his naval counterpart. A clipper-ship ditty of the late 1800's says that to be a real sailor one must have,

Every finger a fish-hook,
Every tooth a marline spike,
Every hair a rope yarn,
Every drop of blood — Stockholm Tar.

It was a tough life indeed, somewhat made up for by the fact that discipline in merchant ships was more lax than in the navy. But even in the merchant service, 'bully-boy' masters and mates were not unknown, and many a sailor was 'started' with a knotted rope's end.

Naval pay, for most of the period covered, was quite good in comparison with wages ashore although the Admiralty was almost always behind in the payment of them. Sometimes years behind. In merchant ships, pay was more prompt, but was lower than in the navy.

The food on board naval ships was often, although not invariably, of poor quality. During some periods, Admiralty contractors used to cheat on both quantity and quality. Water was carried in wooden barrels, and thus quickly became undrinkable, and had to be replenished as often as possible, and in any way possible. This included collecting ice from icebergs, a dangerous practice as we shall see later on in this book.

In the 17th century Pepys was to write,

'Englishmen, and more especially seamen, love their bellies above everything else, and therefore it must always be remembered, in the management of the victualling of the navy, that to make any abatement of them in quantity or agreeableness of their victuals, is to discourage and provoke them in their tenderest point, and will sooner render them disgusted with the King's service than any other hardship that could be put upon them.'

Despite this, that conditions hadn't improved much if at all by 1761 is evidenced by the following written by William Thompson in that year. He entitled it, '*An appeal to the Public to prevent the Navy of England being supplied with pernicious Provisions.*' He said:

'That Mariners in the King's Ships have frequently put their 24 hours allowance of salt provisions into their tobacco boxes. That seamen in the King's Ships have made buttons for their Jackets and Trowses with the Cheese they were served with, having preferred it, by reason of its tough and durable quality, to buttons made of common metal; and that Carpenters in the Navy-Service have made Trucks (i.e. round caps — Author's note) *to their Ship's flagstaffs with whole Cheeses, which have stood the weather equally with any timber. That the Flour in the King's Ships has been devoured by weevils, and became so intolerably musty, and cemented into such hard rocks, that the men have been obliged to use instruments, with all their feeble power, to break and pulverise it before they could make use of it, as though, in a comparitive degree, they had been stubbing to pieces the ruins of an old fortification.*

That their bread has been so full of large black-headed maggots and that they have so nauseated the thoughts of it, as to be obliged to shut their eyes

to confine that sense from being offended before they could bring their minds into a resolution of consuming it.

That their beer has stunk as abominably as the foul stagnant water which is pumped out of many cellars in London at midnight hour; and that they were under a necessity of shutting their eyes, and stopping their breath by holding their noses before they could conquer their aversion, so as to prevail upon themselves in their extreme necessities to drink it'.

(As noted above, that was written in 1761. Just in case the reader may think that by the 20th century, all these conditions were a thing of the past, the author would like to point out that in the late 1940's, he had personal experience of maggots and weevils being found in flour on board tramp vessels he served in. Before making bread from this flour, these little creatures were mostly sieved out!)

In the 18th century the food was not made any better by the supposedly humanitarian practice of giving the post of Cook on board to incapacitated sailors who, by reason of injury, were unfit to do anything else!

Until well into the 19th century diseases were rife on board ships. These included scurvy, typhus and tuberculosis, caused by conditions on the ships themselves, and venereal disease and various fevers brought from ashore.

The scourge of scurvy was caused by lack of vitamin C. The exact cause was unknown until vitamins were 'discovered' in the 20th century. Until then it was thought that 'vapours' from the oceans might have been one of the causes. It has been said that far more seamen died from this disease than were ever killed in battle. On Anson's voyage around the world in 1740-1744, seven out of every eight men who set sail with him died, and mainly from this disease.

Another aspect of life in the navy from the earliest times until well into the 1800's, was impressment — the use of Press Gangs as a recruiting device. However necessary the system was, it had few friends outside the navy, and not a few antagonists within it. The merchant service disliked it, as they made up the largest quota of victims. The Press was mainly on the lookout for trained seamen, and although non-seamen were pressed, such men made up a very small percentage of the total.

Some of the more enlightened naval captains of the 18th century were opposed to its use, and in general it can be said that such captains had rarely to resort to its use, as they could often man their ships, or very nearly so, with volunteers. It is on record that in the year of Trafalgar, some 300 men were pressed at Great Yarmouth.

The merchant service, the main victim of the system, had their own system of recruitment. They used the services of the 'crimp' to lure seamen away from naval ships and other merchant ships, for a payment.

The victims of the press were not always 'ordinary' seamen, and in the case of landsmen, not always from the lower social orders. Mates off merchantmen were often pressed, and sometimes were given warrant positions in the navy. John Newton, who was later to become successively a slave ship captain, a custom's officer, a famous pastor, and the co-author (with William Cowper) of the well known Olney Hymns, was taken by the Press in 1744. His father, a sea-captain, interceded on his behalf, but this served only to get young Newton promoted to midshipman; he was not released. (Later Newton deserted, and when recaught, was demoted and flogged.)

This brings us to another notable aspect of naval life; flogging as a method of punishment. It was used in the navy as late as 1880. It was the most common of all forms of punishment. Some captains misused the system, but this was far from general. By the 1740's, captains were expressly forbidden to order more than 12 lashes; serious crimes liable to stiffer penalties were subject to a court-martial, which could order substantially more. As court-martials were exceedingly difficult to organise, captains tended to ignore the 12 lash maximum penalty, but they could not do so with impunity. Several 'cruel' captains were dismissed the service.

Given the circumstances of life on board naval vessels of the 17th to 19th centuries, it is difficult to see how the use of the lash could have been avoided. In a ship where the 'men' outnumbered the officers by a large proportion, and when the ship was outside the ken of superior authority for long stretches of time, it appears that there was no adequate alternative. As 'leave' was irregular and not granted as an entitlement, the threat of loss of it would have had little effect. There is evidence to suggest that most seamen preferred the lash, providing the number of lashes was within reason, to having their rum ration withdrawn. There is also evidence that suggests that, providing such punishment was kept within certain limits and was applied fairly, the ordinary sailor tended to agree with the system — one supposes this applied in cases where one was not the victim oneself.

(One common misconception needs to be corrected here. For most of the period covered, the admiralty rarely accepted the sweepings of our goals into the service. They would accept persons convicted of smuggling, for they were usually good sailors, and they also accepted persons from the debtor's prisons, but it was rare for them to accept — knowingly — criminals with a more nefarious background. They didn't want to import trouble into their ships.)

Taken all in all, it is of no small wonder that there was always a supply of volunteers to take up a life at sea. Why did such men voluntarily inflict such a life upon themselves? Maybe it was from a sense of adventure, the thrill of being involved in the discovery of new lands, and the chance of visiting exotic old ones. Maybe it was from a love of fighting, the chance of prize money, or a search for glory. In the merchant service, it may have been the chance to share in the profits of a voyage. Or perhaps it was the realisation that, apart from the chance of being killed in battle, life at sea was not much worse for most of the period covered than life ashore.

In the case of officers, the navy was one way for second sons of the nobility, for sons of impecunious gentry, and even sons of people well down the social scale, to make a name for themselves. One did not live on one's salary in the army (a private income was required), but this was not the case in the navy, where many officers did just that.

In the early centuries under review, the art and science of navigation was based on rule-of-thumb methodology. Sailors had for long known how to obtain their latitude (their distance north or south of their point of departure), but without accurate time-keepers, they could not accurately gauge their longitude (their distance east or west of a given meridian). They could only measure the latter roughly, by estimating the distance run on each days sail, and sometimes these estimates were grossly in error. They knew enough, however, usually to ensure that they could find their way back home, and that sufficed in those early days.

As time went on certain improvements were made. The instruments they used were better. In the year 1600, William Gilbert of Norwich published a treatise based on his studies of the lodestone, and the properties of magnetism. (This work is generally considered to be the first English scientific work.) It is doubtful, however, if many seamen studied or learnt much more than the basic rudiments of their craft in those early days.

As we shall see in the section on Captain Collins, the late 17th century brought improvements in British cartography, but it was not until the 18th century with the invention of the chronometer and the machine for accurately cutting the scales on instruments — by Englishmen John Harrison and Jesse Ramsden respectively — that sailing the oceans became much safer than heretofore.

Dr. Johnson could never understand why anyone would wish to take up a sea life. He said it was like being in prison, with the added chance of being drowned. As the prosperity of our nation was built upon the endeavours of our seamen, it is as well that there were always volunteers around who would have disagreed with the good doctor.

Nicholas of Lynn (fl.1340-1380)
King's Lynn

We are all taught at school that Colombus 'discovered' America in 1492 (although he himself thought until his dying day, that he had discovered islands off the east coast of Cathay).

Since very early times there have been legends and myths about other voyagers who may have preceded him, albeit in much higher latitudes. At various times the Irish, the Scots, the English, the Portuguese, the Vikings (to name just some) have taken credit for the discovery of the New World. The only one of these to have been proven is that of the Vikings in the 11th century.

However, many eminent scholars support many other candidates for the honour. St. Brendan and his fellow Irish monks (A.D. 400-600) have their supporters. The Scotsman Prince Henry Sinclair, in company with the Venetian Nicolo Zeno, has his proponents and is supposed to have made a successful American voyage in 1398. The Welsh Prince Madoc is said to have made it 15 years before Colombus. His claims have been mainly propounded by a distinguished Welsh professor. A number of the claims made have a nationalistic fervour attached to them, but the same criticism cannot be levelled at those made on behalf of Nicholas of Lynn. His main supporters are an American and a Russian.

Nicholas of Lynn was a Carmelite monk who lived in the 14th century. He may have studied at Oxford. He was interested in the astrolabe, and may have been the first Englishman to have studied that instrument. He studied astronomy, produced mathematical tables for use in navigation and, at the request of John of Gaunt, computed a calendar for the years 1387 to 1462.

In 1962, the Russian Professor Samuel Varshavesky stated that his studies had led him to the conclusion that Nicholas had voyaged to North America at some time before 1350. Varshavesky said that Nicholas visited the Arctic regions, and the Canadian islands in the vicinity of Labrador. Nicholas is said to have written about his voyage in his book 'De Inventio Fortunata' in 1364. Varshavesky's work is a recapitulation and extension of the thesis put forward by the American Dr. B.F. Da Costa, in the latter part of the 19th century.

A copy of Nicholas' book was presented to King Edward III, at Castle Rising in 1364. It is said that five manuscript copies of this book were in existence between that date and the mid-16th century, but unfortunately none of these can now be traced. (It has been suggested that Colombus had a copy with him on his voyage.) However, references to this book can be found in other documents of that time and later.

Hakluyt mentions the travels of Nicholas in his 'Voyages' (c.1600). Nicholas is reported to have seen floating islands of pumice (from underwater volcanic explosions, and often seen in the waters west of Iceland); he found that the ship's compass didn't work properly in certain areas visited; (there is a large magnetic anomaly in some parts of the eastern Canadian archipelago, caused by huge iron ore deposits.)

Varshavesky puts forward other evidence to show that such a voyage was made, and that Nicholas was the man who made it. His case is quite convincing, and may be proved beyond doubt if ever a copy of the missing book comes to light.

Perhaps it is worth mentioning here, that 'armchair' historians have often refused to believe that any of these early voyages and others like them, could have been made, "because the technology was not available". They often specifically mention the ships that were available to these early mariners, and state that they were entirely unsuited to make long voyages of any kind. Thor Heyerdahl, and Tim Severin, and others like them have now put paid to such statements. A number of these early vessels were very seaworthy indeed, and even if they had not been, there would always have been the adventurous soul, prepared to take a risk, and sail out on just about anything that would float, in the search for new lands, for gold, or for heathens to convert.

Nicholas of Lynn may have preceded Colombus by some 150 years, and may have been the first Englishman to visit the New World. But let us not jump to conclusions, for there is a vague reference to an unnamed Lynn merchant who may have got there in 1271! This is not as surprising as it might appear at first sight, for Lynn had trading connections with Iceland and Norway, both of which traded regularly with the Norse colony in Greenland from its foundation in the late 10th century until its demise in the 15th.

According to tradition, Nicholas is buried in Greyfriars Gardens at King's Lynn.

Thomas Howard, 3rd Duke of Norfolk (1473-1554) Kenninghall

Thomas Howard held a number of high offices under Henry VIII, including that of Lord High Admiral. In 1520 he was in command of a fleet sent against the French. He was also a General of the Army, and earlier, in 1513, had been at the rout of the Scots at Flodden Field.

He was uncle to two of Henry's six wives, Anne Boleyn and Catherine Howard. (There is a persistent legend in the area, that Anne's body was secretly buried in the Salle Churchyard.) Upon the execution of the latter, Thomas lost a great deal of his power, and four years later he was accused of being an accessory to treason and condemned to death. He was lucky — Henry died just before the sentence was due to be carried out. He stayed imprisoned during the short reign of Edward VI, but was released when Mary came to the throne in 1553.

Howard had built a magnificent house at Kenninghall. During his period of 'disgrace', this had been settled on the then Princess Mary. The house, together with his other estates and his dukedom, were returned to him on Mary's accession. He died in the house in August 1554.

The house was pulled down in the 17th century. There is only a fragment of it left. It is of red brick, with blue lozenges set in them as a surface decoration.

Clement Paston (c.1515-1597)
Oxnead

The family that produced the Paston Letters, several judges and sheriffs, some distinguished soldiers and knights, also produced one sea captain of note.

Clement Paston was born at Paston circa 1515, and has been variously described as being either the second or the fourth son of Sir William Paston. Little is known of his youth apart from the fact that he spent part of it fighting in France. His abilities must have impressed Henry VIII, for Clement was made a pensioner and called *'a fitting man to command a king's ship'*. (A pensioner was a gentleman-at-arms on some sort of stipend from the king.) In 1545, he was given command of the *Pelican* of Danzig, in a fleet under the Lord Lisle. In the following year, possibly still in that same ship, he captured the *Galley Blancherd* which was added to the English navy as the *Mermaid.* Captured with the galley was the Admiral of France, Baron St. Blancerd, who was brought to England as a captive and held at Caister-nigh-Yarmouth. A ransom of 7000 crowns was eventually paid for him. Clement kept the plunder from the galley, which included a snake-handled gold cup which became a Paston family heirloom.

Tomb of Clement Paston, Oxnead

In 1547, at the Battle of Pinkie, in Scotland, he was wounded and left for dead on the field. In Clement Paston we find a good example of that fighting duality that was to last for at least another 100 years, wherein there was no distinction between the land based warrior, and the ship based one. There was no separate army and navy as we know them today. Even the ships were constructed as if they were floating castles with, fore and aft, high superstructures from which to fire down on the enemy. (The bow structure of a ship is to this day called the forecastle or fo'c'sle.)

Clement survived his wounds however, and later resided at Newhaven where he commanded some of Queen Elizabeth's ships. His rhyming epitaph states that he served four sovereigns, *'sometime by sea and sometime on the shore'*.

He lived out his old age in the county of his birth. In 1570, he became a magistrate, and later, deputy-lieutenant. In 1588, he was sheriff of Norfolk. It was said that he was lukewarm on the subject of religion, but he must have been a kindly man for he built an hospice at Oxnead for six deserving poor men.

He had earlier married Alice, widow of one Edward Lambert. Her maiden name was Packington. There appears not to have been any issue from this marriage, as his will left the larger part of his property to his wife, and the remainder to his nephew. Clement died on 18th February 1597. He is buried in a marble tomb in the tiny and tree-hidden Church of St. Michael at Oxnead.

In the early 18th century the family home of the Pastons, Oxnead Hall, which Clement had built, together with its estates, was sold to Admiral Lord George Anson.

In Paston's time, naval tactics and armaments were just beginning to emerge from their mediaeval stage, a stage where sea-battles were fought exactly as a land-battle would have been fought. The changes were slow to develop, but gradually ships became more streamlined, guns were improved, and tactics were changed. By the middle of the 16th century tactics had got beyond the stage of manoeuvering one's vessel to windward of the enemy, and then throwing cannisters of quicklime at him, but what may be termed the floating castle syndrome took a long time to die out.

Philip Gawdy (1562-1617)
Redenhall

A gallant and famous sea battle was fought in 1591. It has since fired the imagination and patriotism of generations of English schoolboys. It has been called the Battle of the Azores, and in it, the solitary *Revenge*, under the command of Sir Richard Grenville, engaged an entire Spanish battle-fleet. Amongst the crew of the *Revenge* was a scion of the Norfolk family called Gawdy.

The Gawdys, much like the Pastons and the Heydons, were a Norfolk family which experienced a period of importance followed by a sudden fall into near oblivion. In the case of the Gawdys, their period of greatness lasted for about 200 years.

They were a family of lawyers, sheriffs, and parsons, and they had their heyday in the 16th and 17th centuries. Their fortune and fame came from the success of three half-brothers, each of whom attained high office in the legal profession. One became Recorder of Norwich and Lynn, another a Justice of the Queen's Bench, and the third, Chief Justice of the Common Pleas. The family, through cleverly arranged marriages, made important connections (together with concomitant land acquisitions) all over the County.

Philip Gawdy, lawyer, courtier, and sailor was the grandson of Sir Thomas Gawdy of Redenhall, Justice of the Queen's Bench. Philip was born on 13th July 1562, probably at West Harling. At the age of sixteen he was admitted to the Inner Temple. Apparently he did not take his early career too seriously, for it is reported that he spent a good deal of his time learning to play the lute.

He became M.P. for Thetford in the year of the Armada, 1588, and remained so for five years. It was during this period that he took part in the Battle of the Azores.

In the summer of 1591, an English squadron of fifteen ships under Lord Thomas Howard, who flew his flag in the *Defiance*, was despatched to the Azores with orders to intercept the Spanish treasure fleet from the West Indies. Philip served first in the *Defiance* and then transferred to the *Revenge*.

The English waited in vain for the treasure fleet to appear. Instead, they were surprised by a fleet of fifty-three Spanish men-of-war. The English squadron retreated, except for the *Revenge*.

No one knows why Grenville decided to stay and fight. Some historians say that he stayed in order to pick up some of his men who were on shore. Others say that he may have been glory hunting. Either theory would fit in with what we know of Sir Richard's character. Whatever the reason, stay he did. His one ship with 150 men on board, fought one-by-one, fifteen Spanish galleons with a combined complement of 5,000 men. He sank two of the Spanish ships in a battle which lasted for fifteen hours. Grenville only struck his flag after the last barrel of powder had been expended. Forty Englishmen lay dead, and Grenville himself was amongst the severely wounded. He died two days later, and the battered *Revenge* was soon to sink in a storm.

The Spaniards treated the survivors, Philip Gawdy among them, with great

Ship from the Gawdy chest, Redenhall

Ship from the Gawdy chest, Redenhall

honour. They were shipped to Portugal, though some were lost when the ships transporting them foundered in a storm. Philip survived to be imprisoned in Lisbon Castle. He was ransomed for the then considerable sum of £200 by his brother, Sir Bassingborne Gawdy.

Throughout his life, Philip was a voluminous letter writer, and one with a nice turn of phrase. His many letters to friends and relations provide a colourful account of his career, and show his love for the county of his birth. He must have had more than his fair share of the spirit of adventure. Writing just before the last battle of the *Revenge*, he said, *"We stay and pray every day heartily for the Spanish fleet coming"*. Later he wrote, *"I may justly say that I have travelled farther than any of my name"*.

Philip Gawdy's later career included periods as M.P. for Eye, Thetford again, for Sudbury, and then for Dunwich. He was appointed undersheriff for Norfolk in 1609 and married Bridget Strangman circa 1597. He died in London in 1617.

He once wrote, *"And when I think of Norfolk ... I sighe and saye the sea doth not content me"*. One wonders how many other Norfolk seamen down the years have had similar thoughts, and whether there was one among them who could have phrased the notion better.

There is a Gawdy Chapel in Redenhall Church. Nearby Gawdy Hall was demolished early in this century, and a Venetian chest dating from about 1450, was removed from the chapel at the Hall, to its present place in the church. The chest is made from cypress wood, and has paintings of ships on the inside of the lid, which gives it considerable rarity value.

William Harborne (d.1617)
Great Yarmouth

William Harborne, trader, traveller and the first English ambassador to the Ottoman Empire, was born at Great Yarmouth which had been a port of considerable importance for centuries. (The records for the year 1347 show that 190 ships of between 40 and 100 tons were registered at the port in addition to some 250 fishing boats. By 1611 the mapmaker John Speed could write that *"At Yarmouth every year in September is the worthiest herring fishery in Europe, which draweth a concourse of people and maketh the town much richer all the year".*) We know that Harborne was one of the bailiffs of this thriving port in 1572, and that he was a factor in Spain before becoming a founder member of the Spanish Company in 1577.

He travelled to Turkey in 1578, going by sea to Hamburg, and then journeying across Europe to Constantinople. That journey took him four months, a measure of the difficulties of travel in Elizabethan times and, for that matter, for some considerable time thereafter. Although the journey was made primarily for commercial purposes, there was some element of state interest in his contacts. England was always seeking ways of gaining political advantage from trading arrangements. In this case, England was fast approaching a time of conflict with Spain and, in the Mediterranean, that country's main enemy were the Turks.

Harborne seems to have impressed the sultan. That potentate appeared eager to invite the friendship of the Queen of England, and he granted safe-conduct to any English merchant who wished to trade within his territory. Harborne also managed to obtain the release of many English captives serving as slaves in Turkish galleys.

Back home, and as a result of Harborne's visit, the joint-stock Turkey Company was set up in 1579. It is likely that Harborne had some contact with his fellow Norfolkman, John Eldred, over this matter. In 1582, William was formally appointed ambassador to Turkey, and stayed in that country until 1588. His activities there were extremely successful. English merchants procured more trade from the Turkish empire than any other nation. This greatly pleased Queen Elizabeth, as it significantly increased the amount of import customs duties that went into her coffers. She was always short of money, and any increase in her funds was always gratefully received.

In hyperbolic terms in 1598, it was written that the *'mercurial-breasted Mr. Harborne who always accepted a rich spark of eternity, first lighted and inkindled at Yarmouth ... who ... hath ... noised the name of our island and of Yarmouth, so tritonly, that not an infant of the ... Pagans, but talk of London as frequently as of their Prophet's tomb at Mecca'.*

There is no record of Harborne making a large fortune out of his trading activities. Neither did he earn much from the Queen as her ambassador. One thing he did earn was the undying gratitude of the many men he had released from the torments of the Ottoman galleys.

He settled at Mundham, Norfolk, and died there in 1617. He is buried under the main aisle of the Church of St. Peter, Mundham.

John Eldred (1552-1632)
New Buckenham

John Eldred was born at New Buckenham, Norfolk, in 1552, and at an early age went to London, set up as a merchant there, and made a great deal of money. *'Upon Shrove Monday 1583'*, according to the account of his journey published in Hakluyt's 'Voyages', he embarked with several other merchants on a ship called the *Tiger* bound for the Levant. (One of his fellow travellers was Ralph Fitch, who was to make an even more celebrated journey.) When the ship arrived at Tripoli the merchants split up into small groups, each of which proceeded on a designated trading trip.

Eldred went to Aleppo, Baghdad, and Basra. In the latter place he stayed six months, and trade was so good there that the commodities they bought and bartered for filled seventy barges on the upriver return trip to Baghdad. The main commodity was spices. At Baghdad, the goods were loaded on to camels for the journey back to Aleppo. For this trek, they joined a caravan of over 4,000 of these beasts.

Eldred used Aleppo as a base for several other trading trips before embarking on the *Hercules* for London in 1587. When the ship arrived home it was said that it '*was the richest ship of . . . goods that was ever known to come into this realm*'. A goodly part of the entire cargo belonged to Eldred. He thus moved up from being merely rich, to being extremely rich. He continued to reside mainly in London, but bought a huge estate at Great Saxham in Suffolk, and built a large house there. The locals called the house 'Nutmeg Hall'.

He expanded his business interests. He was one of the pioneers of the Turkey Company, a group of Merchant Venturers set up to trade with that country. In 1602, he sent the *Mayflower* and three other vessels on a trading voyage to the West Indies.

The East India Company was set up on 31st December 1600, and John Eldred was one of its leaders, and was a member of its first court of directors. This company existed for over two hundred and fifty years, and during that time grew from a joint stock company interested mainly in spices, to an organisation that held sway over a vast mercantile empire, and which ruled many parts of British India for a good part of that period.

The company eventually had its own fleet of ships that were virtually indistinguishable from navy ships, and in some cases were better armed and manned than naval vessels of the same size. The company's ships often took part in official government expeditions in consort with ships of the navy. This happened in 1792, on the occasion of the first embassy of Great Britain to the Emperor of China, and in the 19th century, East India Company ships assisted the navy in its fights against pirates in Borneo waters. The ships, although officially classed as merchantmen, were run very much on naval lines.

The company had its own armies. It engaged in wars, and over the years expanded its areas of influence, especially in India. It was not until 1773, when it got into some financial difficulty, that the incongruity of a merchant company having its own empire and the wherewithal to maintain it hit home, and by The Regulating Act passed by the British Parliament, the company ceased to be an autonomous body. (The Dutch East India Company, in contrast, had always been very much a government concern.)

John Eldred did not see all this development take place, of course, but he played a very prominent role in its early affairs. He must have been extremely industrious, for he didn't stop there. In 1606, he was involved in the setting up of the company granted the right to colonize lands in the Chesapeake Bay area, in defiance of Spain's monopoly of the New World, a monopoly which dated back to the Treaty of Tordesillas of 1494. Eldred did not like the Spanish. In 1603 two of his vessels had been captured by them, and another fell into their hands in 1606. In each case the prisoners taken were apparently treated with extreme cruelty.

Eldred had married soon after his return from the Levant, and he sired a large family. One of his sons was made a baronet in 1641. Eldred himself died at his Great Saxham estate in 1632. There is a monument to him in the church there. However, he may have a more significant memorial than that which may outlast the stone one. It is thought that Shakespeare must have had the story in Hakluyt's 'Voyages' in mind when he penned the following lines in 'Macbeth': *'Her husband's to Aleppo gone, master o'the Tiger.'*

John Rolfe (1585-1622)
Heacham

In the year 1958, the wreck of an early 17th century ship was found in an underwater search off the Bermudas. Since 1978, a small but well organised archaeological expedition has been working on the site of the wreck. It's importance lies in the fact that it is the earliest known find of an English trading vessel. It is the wreck of the *Sea Adventure*, which struck a reef in 1609.

The ship had sailed from England in June 1609, as part of a nine ship fleet, carrying colonists for Virginia. The voyage had been organised by the Virginia Company, of which John Eldred of New Buckenham was one of the principal backers. The *Sea Adventure* was the flagship, and Sir George Somers was the captain and overall commander. With him on the flagship sailed Sir Thomas Gates, the new lieutenant-governor of the colony, William Strachey, secretary, and John Rolfe from Heacham.

William Strachey was to write that they met with a great storm that lasted for seven days. It separated them from the rest of the fleet, and blew them away from Cape Henry, Virginia. It finally set them up on a reef on what he called Devil's Island but all the people on the ship were saved. Strachey's account of the wreck is thought to have been the pattern for Shakespeare's 'Tempest'.

John Rolfe came from a well-known West Norfolk family, who lived at Heacham Hall. He was baptised in Heacham Church on the 6th May 1585. He married in 1608, and his wife was pregnant when they boarded the *Sea Adventure* together. The Rolfe child was born on the shipwreck island but died in infancy.

From some of the timbers of the wrecked vessel, the crew managed to build two small pinnaces. One of these was named the *Deliverance*. In these craft, they eventually reached Virginia in May 1610. They found the settlement in a state of strife and sickness, with relations with the local Indians anything but good.

Over a period Rolfe became one of the leading men of the settlement. After considerable trial and error, he became the first of them successfully to cultivate a marketable tobacco. His wife died there, and he remarried in 1613. This lady's name was Pocahontas, often described as an Indian Princess. She was the daughter of the most important Indian chief in the area, Powhatan.

It was she who had saved the life of Captain John Smith in 1607. (Smith is often said to have been born at King's Lynn. He was in fact from Lincolnshire, although he had connections with Lynn.) The Indians were going to kill Smith, but Pocahontas threw herself between him and his potential murderers. This tale has been embellished with romantic interest, but even given the comparatively early nubility of Indian maidens, there must be some doubt about this, as she was only 11 or 12 years old at the time.

In 1616, John Rolfe and Pocahontas (now a Christian and renamed Rebecca) together with their child, came to England. Pocahontas — this author refuses to call her Rebecca! — became something of a celebrity. She was presented at court and had her portrait painted. Unfortunately, the English weather did not agree with her, and almost on the eve of her departure back to America, she died in March 1617. She was buried in the chancel of St. George's Church, Gravesend.

Rolfe subsequently married again, and returned to Virginia where he died in 1622. His son by the princess, called Thomas, was raised by Henry Rolfe, a kinsman who lived in London. Thomas returned to Virginia in 1640, married and had a daughter. She had many descendants.

Many are the legends that have been built around the stories of Pocahontas and Smith, and Pocahontas and Rolfe. One of the latter states that Rolfe married the princess for the well-being of the plantation in that it improved relations with the Indians. As she is reported to have been a lady of rare grace and beauty, it is likely that those factors were far more important in the mind of the young widower, than any 'for the good of all' hypothesis. In the vernacular of today, he probably just fancied her!

Vice-Admiral Sir Christopher Myngs (1625-1666) Salthouse

Sir Christopher Myngs lived through the period of the English Civil War, the Commonwealth, and the Restoration. He was the first of that triumvirate of North Norfolk admirals, each of whom played an important part in the navy of the day. It is thought that the three, (the other two being Sir John Narborough and Sir Cloudesley Shovell), may have been kinsmen. It is certain that Myngs aided Narborough in his career, and Narborough later did the same for Shovell.

All three were examples of 'tarpaulin captains', men who had risen by experience and competence through the ranks of the navy. There was always rivalry, and sometimes considerable bitterness, between that group and the 'gentlemen captains' who were given their positions for patronage reasons. In Myngs case, as we shall see, it is likely that he belonged to that even rarer breed of naval commanders of the time, whose men would have followed him anywhere.

Samuel Pepys makes several references to Myngs in his diary. Some of the information he recorded on Myngs' family background is probably inaccurate. He has him coming from a humble family, with a shoemaker father. This is at variance with the few known facts, and also at variance with the traditional information about Myngs available in the Salthouse area.

His father, John Myngs, was a near kinsman of Nicolas Mynnes of a well-known old Norfolk family. He may well have been a son. (Christopher Myngs himself, seems to have adopted the spelling of the family name used here.) His mother was Katherine Parr, daughter of Christopher Parr, a landowner in the Kelling area of North Norfolk.

Myngs was baptised at Salthouse in November 1625. We know nothing of his early childhood, but it is likely that he took up a sea career at an early age, possibly in the coastal trade of East Anglia. At some time during the mid-1640's, he joined one of the state's ships. In 1652, we hear of him aboard the *Elizabeth* in a Mediterranean squadron under Commodore Richard Badiley. In the following year Myngs was promoted to command of the *Elizabeth* when its captain was killed in an action against the Dutch.

Under Myngs this ship was later engaged in meritorious service in the Channel and Home waters. On one occasion, after he had been instrumental in capturing a number of Dutch ships, his services were ordered by parliament 'to be noted by the Council of State'.

He then saw several years service in West Indian waters, and during one short break in this, he married his first wife in England in 1657. At the time of the Restoration in 1660 he was still in the West Indies, so was largely unaffected by the event. According to Pepys, Myngs '*came into great renown*' during this period of service, although we have few details of it.

In 1664, he was promoted to vice-admiral, and hoisted his flag in the *Royal Oak*. The ship was part of the Channel squadron under the overall command of Prince Rupert. He then transferred to the *Triumph* in a fleet under the Duke of York. On the 3rd June 1665, Myngs took part in the Battle of Lowestoft, the opening naval battle of the Second Dutch War. The battle ended in a decisive victory for the English when the Dutch flagship *Eendracht* blew up after receiving a direct hit in the powder-room. She had a crew of over 400, and only five of them were saved. In all, the Dutch lost over thirty ships, against a loss of two for the English. Later in the same month Christopher Myngs was knighted for his services in the battle.

Sir Christopher Myngs
(National Maritime Museum, London)

The Duke of York commissioned Sir Peter Lely to paint portraits of all the commanders who took part in that battle, and the portrait of Sir Christopher from which our illustration is taken, was one of them.

Following that battle Myngs was in command of a squadron guarding the Channel trade routes. His work here was commended on several occasions.

In April 1666, Sir Christopher hoisted his flag in the *Victory*, and so became the first Norfolk admiral to be connected with a ship of that name. (It was not, of course, the same ship. Nelson's *Victory* was launched in 1765.)

During the first four days of June 1666, the Dutch and English fleets fought one of the longest and most hard-fought battles in history. The English suffered a severe defeat, losing seventeen ships and 8,000 men. This defeat was to be reversed only seven weeks later at the Battle of Orfordness, but Myngs was not to live to see it.

The *Victory* along with the rest of Prince Rupert's squadron, had been detached from the main English fleet, and so did not take part in the first three days fighting of what is now called The Four Days' Battle. They arrived on the fourth day, and Myngs led the van of the red squadron. During fierce fighting, he was shot through the throat. He refused to leave the deck for treatment, and held the lips of the wound together with his fingers. Another bullet passed through his neck, and he fell to the deck. He thus became the first of the two British admirals of Norfolk extraction to be shot and mortally wounded aboard a ship called the *Victory*.

Pepys attended the funeral which took place in London on June 13th. It is thought that Myngs died from his wounds a few days before this at his Whitechapel residence. In his diary, Pepys recorded the following, which indicates the affection that seamen had for the dead admiral. He described how, '*about a dozen able, lusty, proper men came to the coach side with tears in their eyes, and one of them, that spoke for the rest, said ... "We are here a dozen of us that have long known and loved and served our dead commander, Sir Christopher Myngs, and have now done the last office of laying him in the ground. We would be glad we had any other to offer after him and in revenge of him. All we have is our lives; if you will please to get his Royal Highness to give us a fireship among us all, choose you one to be commander, and the rest of us, whoever he is, will serve him, and if possible, do that that shall show our memory of our dead commander and our revenge"*. This was honour indeed, for the mortality rate in a fireship operation was exceedingly high, and captured survivors from them were often executed out of hand.

Sir Christopher Myngs was survived by his second wife Rebecca, and by their son. A daughter, Mary, by his first wife also survived him. To her he left in his will the sum of £300. A copy of this will can be seen in St. Nicholas Church, Salthouse. Mary Myngs is buried under a ledger stone in that church. (Next to Mary's grave, there is a memorial to the Stanforth family. A Margaret Stanforth was to marry the Reverend Dixon Hoste in about the year 1775. One of their six sons was to become a protégé of Nelson, Captain Sir William Hoste.)

Myngs' son by his second wife, who was also named Christopher, followed his father into the navy. He commanded the *Namur* at the Battle of Malaga in 1704 and later became a commissioner of the navy at Portsmouth. He died in 1725.

Admiral Sir John Narborough (1640-1688) Cockthorpe

John Narborough was baptised in Cockthorpe Church on the 11th October 1640. His pickled bowels, together with other internal organs, were buried in Knowlton Church near Deal in Kent, in 1688.

Narborough is one of the most interesting of Norfolk seamen. Through him, as we shall see, there are connections with other seamen from the county. He was to die whilst taking part in a semi-official sunken treasure hunt, and his participation in that affair was to result in a sensational piece of archaeological detection work in 1978.

He was the son of Gregory Narbrough (another way of spelling his name), and may have been some sort of relation to Sir Christopher Myngs. He probably started his sea career in the merchant service, but later sailed with Myngs to the West Indies. It was during this period that, in a very junior capacity on board Myngs' ship, he was involved in his first hunt for the sunken treasure which was to be the main occupation of the last months of his life. On this occasion the hunt was unsuccessful.

Narborough was a lieutenant in 1664 and for the next two years followed Myngs into successive ships. He was at the Battle of Lowestoft in 1665, and was on board the *Victory* in 1666, when Myngs was fatally wounded. His conduct during that battle must have impressed his superiors, for immediately after it he was given command of the *Assurance.*

In that ship he took part in the West Indies campaign against both the Dutch and the French. At Surinam, he was wounded in the right thigh by a musket ball. This injury may have left him with a permanent limp. He also contracted fever there — a common enough occurence on that least popular of all the naval stations. Narborough was a great believer in bleeding as a preventative against tropical fevers, and once wrote, "... *when I come near the Equinoctial I always breathed a vein*".

In 1669 he was given command of a two-ship expedition to the 'South Seas', with orders to make a survey of the north west coast of America. He was also ordered to attempt to break the Spanish monopoly of trade on the west coast of South America, a difficult enough task for two small ships and about a hundred men. The ships were the *Sweepstakes* and the *Bachelor.*

The captain of the *Bachelor* left the expedition without permission before the ships reached the Magellan Straits, and returned home with the story that Narborough's ship had been lost in a storm. Without the stores carried by the other vessel, Narborough had no chance at all of carrying out his orders, but at least he tried.

He passed through the Straits, charting them as he went. In this, he was probably aided by the master, Grenville Collins of Cley-next-the-Sea. (A copy of Narborough's journal containing sailing directions for the Straits was carried on board the *Wager*, one of Anson's vessels on his circumnavigation in 1740-1744, and when that ship was wrecked, it helped the crew extricate themselves from

The Battle of Lowestoft, 1665
(National Maritime Museum, London)

an extremely dangerous situation.)

He sailed northward up the Chilean coast, but at Valdivia, four of his men were detained by the port authorities there. As he did not have sufficient men to attempt a rescue, he decided to return home. (One of the four men left behind was Lieut. Thomas Armiger, aged 40, and a Norfolk man. He married a local woman at Valdivia, and lived there for sixteen years. He was then charged with treason and executed. There is no record of what happened to the other three.) James Burney, writing about 1803, criticised Narborough for abandoning these men, but in the circumstances it would appear that there was no alternative.

The *Sweepstakes* arrived back home in June 1671. The expedition had not accomplished its aims but Narborough gained in reputation, not least because of the care he showed for the health of his men. He insisted that everyone on board, officers and men, had the same allowances, and his standing orders to the captain of the *Bachelor* had included the injunction *"to have your Ship kept sweet and clean for the preservation of your men's health"*. He was to keep this reputation for the remainder of his life, and on one occasion was officially reprimanded for not reducing his men's food allowances, when according to instructions he should have done so.

In 1672, Narborough was in the flagship *Prince* of the Duke of York, at the Battle of Sole Bay (sometimes called the Battle of Southwold). This was the opening battle of the Third Dutch War. It did not end in a decisive victory for either side, but it did prevent the Anglo-French forces from invading Holland.

Towards the end of 1672, Narborough was sent in the *Fairfax*, and in charge of a small squadron of five ships, to the Mediterranean on convoy duty. On the way back in May of the following year, his fleet almost ran up on the Bishop rocks in the Scillies. One of his officers was Cloudesley Shovell who, as an admiral thirty five years later, was to hit those same rocks with disastrous consequences.

He had arrived back in time to take part in the Battle of the Texel. He was flag captain to Lord Ossory aboard the *St. Michael*. This was possibly the most fiercely fought of all the battles in these wars with the Dutch, and although the result can fairly be called a draw, as no ships were lost on either side, the Dutch had once more put paid to any plans for the invasion of their country.

The English had learnt a good deal from these battles with the Dutch. Narborough wrote in his journal, *"The enemy shoots much more shot than we do, and ply their guns faster; they shoot much pound shot, which fly so thick and cut our rigging so much. When the enemy came near us, I could perceive our shot were well placed in them, but when they were at any distance, our shot often fell short"*. The lessons were hard learned, but once taken in put England on the way to eventual domination of the seas.

Narborough had once again impressed his superiors, and for his services during the battle he was promoted to rear-admiral of the red, and was knighted by the king at Whitehall.

He was sent to the Mediterranean in command of a fleet and, during his four years there, conducted the campaign against the Tripoli and Algerine pirates.

He had a touch of recklessness in his nature, a characteristic which ensured that his men would follow him anywhere. On more than one occasion he personally led his men on shore raiding parties.

Back home in 1677, Narborough married his first wife. She was to die a year later, *"mightily afflicted with a cough, and big with child"*. He was made a Commissioner of the Navy in 1680, and held that post until the year of his death. In that position he gained the confidence of the Secretary of the Navy, Samuel Pepys. The two men worked very closely together in their endeavours to promote the principles of professionalism in the service. Narborough is mentioned several times in Pepys' Diary, and most of the references are complimentary. One of them is not.

The Mediterranean fleet of the time had become a sort of unofficial and private trading organisation, with His Majesty's captains vying with merchant ships and with each other to obtain valuable cargoes to transport home. Every senior person involved, from the admirals downward, received rake-offs, and it was thought that Narborough had taken a few 'gifts' out of this kitty. Pepys, who at one time had not been adverse to taking the occasional back-hander himself, now did his best to stamp out the practice. As the saying goes, 'there is no one holier than the newly converted'.

Narborough's main duties as a Commissioner were concerned with victualling. He did a great deal towards sorting out many of the problems concerned with supplies to the fleet, and in putting the transactions of the department concerned on a sound and businesslike basis.

In 1681, he married again. His second wife was Elizabeth Hill of Shadwell. With part of his wife's dowry he purchased Knowlton Court, and several other estates in Kent. His wife presented him with five children, but only three — two sons and a daughter — survived him.

Now we come to the sunken treasure hunt, and to Narborough's connection with it, which culminated in 1978.

In 1641, a Spanish galleon called the *Nuesta Senora de la Limpia y Pura Concepcion* (from henceforth we shall refer to her as the *Concepcion*) struck a reef north of Hispaniola in the West Indies, and sank. She was reputed to be carrying one of the richest cargoes of treasure ever to leave the Spanish Main. Almost at once, various attempts were made to find her and salvage her cargo. The Spaniards looked for her, as did many of the pirates that operated in the area. Ships of other nations joined in the search; as we have noted above, the young Narborough had served on one of these. However, they all searched in vain.

Then in 1686, a New England sea captain named William Phipps (who later became Sir William and a not too successful Governor of Massachusetts), somehow gained information regarding the location of the *Concepcion*. He sailed to England and set about getting some high officials interested in his project to find the wreck. His information must have been impressive, for a small stock-company of Gentlemen Adventurers was set up. The shareholders included the Duke of Albemarle and John Narborough and, for a percentage of any accruing profits from the venture, the king permitted the use of two small naval ships for the expedition. They were the *James and Mary*, and the *Henry*. Phips commanded one vessel and a certain Francis Rogers, the other.

They found the wreck, and Rogers aboard the *Henry* described the precise location of it in the ship's log. They returned to England with over a quarter of a million pounds sterling, in coin, plate, ingots, and gems. For an investment of £300, Narborough's share came to £32,000! There was still a lot of treasure to be recovered, and gold fever became widespread amongst the higher echelons of both government and navy. On June 14th 1687, some of the Gentlemen Adventurers waited on the King in Council. Samuel Pepys was in attendance to keep the minutes. The meeting resulted in the Adventurers being given the use of the frigate *Foresight*, together with the services of Sir John Narborough to command this second treasure hunt. There was no way, after the rich pickings of the first, that the powers-that-be were going to let the control of this one out of their hands.

However, this time they were not nearly so lucky. Other treasure hunters had taken the easily accessible treasure, and what was left was encased in fifty years of coral growth. The haul was disappointingly small, and in the middle of all this, Sir John Narborough died of fever on the 27th May 1688. He was buried at sea, minus his bowels and other internal organs, which were pickled and brought home for burial.

Along with his entrails, a number of his personal effects were brought back to England. Amongst them was the little log book of the *Henry*, that had been kept so assiduously by its captain, and which contained the exact location of the *Concepcion*. This book ended up in the possession of Sir Robert Marsham who became the first Baron Romney, and finally disappeared into the archives of the Earls of Romney at Gayton Hall, near King's Lynn. There it remained hidden for 300 years.

Over the intervening centuries the treasure of the *Concepcion* never lost its attraction for treasure hunters, but the secret of its location had been lost. None of the searches was successful.

Then, in 1977, a Pennsylvannian named Burt Webber started searching, and he too had no luck. A few years before that, a collection of the Romney family papers were handed over to the Kent County Council, and the *Henry* log book was noted in the catalogue that was produced. In mid-1978, just as he was about to give up the search, this information came to the notice of Webber in a fortuitous and accidental manner, in a letter from a friend. By the end of that year, more of the treasure that Sir John had lost his life looking for was brought to the surface. Tens of millions of dollars of it.

Narborough's death was a sad blow to the navy. There were not too many admirals around with his experience of sea command. James II recognised his worth and honoured his memory by granting Narborough's four year old son John a baronetcy. It was one of the king's last acts before he fled the country in the face of the Glorious Revolution.

Pepys mourned the admiral. He wrote, "*not for private friendship's sake only ... but for the sake of the King and his Service, in which ... I do not think there does survive one superior, if anyone equal ... to Sir John Narborough*".

Capt. Grenville Collins (d.1694)
Cley-next-the-Sea

It is a pity that more is not known of this naval officer, for he was responsible for producing the first English made charts of our coasts. We do know that he was born in the Cley area.

He was master of the *Sweepstakes* under Sir John Narborough on the voyage into the Pacific in 1669-1671 and had this to say about the conduct of the consort ship *Bachelor: "In the year 1669 I had the honour to be with Sir John Narborough in the South Seas, whose noble design was most unfortunately frustrated by the cowardice of our consort, who most basely left us in a Storm before we got to the Straits of Magellan"*. He went on to say that had this not happened, the ships would have followed instructions and gone on to explore the west coast of North America.

Collins was with Narborough again in 1677 in the Mediterranean in the campaign against pirates. He was still serving in the capacity of master.

Four years later he was made Younger Brother of Trinity House and, in that same year, through the offices of Narborough and Samuel Pepys, he was made Hydrographer to the King. (This should not be confused with the post of Hydrographer to the Navy which was not created until 1795.) The Admiralty then commissioned him for the task of charting the coast of Great Britain.

This task had become vital. For a long time, English mariners had had to rely on charts produced by the Dutch. Between the years 1652 and 1674, England and Holland fought three wars with each other, and it seemed illogical in view of the commercial rivalry which had brought about those wars, that the English should have to rely on charts of their own backyard produced by a nation which was intermittently unfriendly.

Collins was provided with two yachts for the purpose. With a compass, a leadline, a measuring chain, and not much else, he set about this work. For most of the time, the operation was inadequately funded. There was no system of triangulation points to help him. Nevertheless, over the next seven years, Collins and his crews produced 120 plans of harbours and coastlines. They were 'plane' charts, and contained many inaccuracies, but they were far better than anything that had been available previously.

48 of them were engraved and made into an atlas first published in 1693. The folio was called 'Great Britain's Coasting Pilot', and went into many editions. (It was first printed by one Freeman Collins, who may have been a brother.)

It was still being issued a 100 years later with only a few changes and was a notable milestone in British cartography, with Grenville Collins lighting the way for later, albeit greater, practitioners of the art like Cook, Vancouver, and Matthew Flinders.

Admiral Sir Cloudesley Shovell (1650-1707) Cockthorpe

In the Great Storm off the British coast of November 1703, thirteen naval ships and about 1500 men were lost. One of the ships involved in that tempest, but which survived to sail another day, was the *Association*. A three-decked ship carrying 90 guns, she was part of Sir Cloudesley Shovell's squadron proceeding to Chatham to lay up for the winter. On this occasion she carried the flag of Vice-Admiral Sir Stafford Fairborne.

The storm drove her clean over the Galloper Bank off Harwich, and towards the Dutch coast. Then the wind backed and drove her north, with the crew expecting every moment to be their last. She managed to anchor off the Elbe, but then another storm blew her north again, and by this time, the damage she had sustained had put her in a dangerous condition. She sought assistance at Copenhagen, and some two months after the Great Storm had raged, she finally made the Medway. That time she had been lucky.

On the 29th September 1707, the *Association*, now flying the flag of Admiral Shovell himself, left Gibraltar to return home in company with twenty other ships.

With no chronometers (it was to be another thirty years before John Harrison produced the first one), and with the inaccurate compasses of the time, navigation was as usual difficult. It was made more difficult this time by the haze they experienced, which made 'shooting' the sun impossible. So, in addition to the usual problem of not knowing their longitude, they did not know their latitude either. The approaches to the Channel had always proved problematic for navigators. Over the years many captains had noted that their vessels had set farther northward than their reckoning had indicated. (We now know that this was caused by a current, called the Rennell Current, which sets northward across the jaws of the Channel, but this was unknown in 1707.)

On October 21st, leadlines indicated that they had 'come into soundings', and Shovell called a conference aboard the flagship to try and determine where they were. It was decided that they were off the coast of France. Only one of the sailing masters involved differed greatly from the near consensus. He was master of the *Lenox*, and he was convinced that the fleet was close to the Scilly Islands. As it turned out, on this occasion anyway, he was the finest navigator of the lot.

The weather became worse, and on the night of the 22nd, the *Association*, together with two other ships-of-the-line, the *Eagle* and the *Romney*, and the fireship *Firebrand*, piled into the Gilstone Rocks off the Scillies, and sank. The remainder of the fleet managed to avoid disaster, although two more ships struck reefs but managed to get themselves off. Over 1400 men were lost that night, making it the second worst peacetime disaster in British naval history, and in it the navy had lost one of the most able admirals of the time.

Sir Cloudesley Shovell's body was washed ashore at Porthellik Cove, and was eventually found half buried in the sand. Two hundred and fifty nine years later, and appropriately enough by a naval sub-aqua club, the remains of his ship were found close to the reef she had hit.

Almost from the moment of the disaster, stories and legends about it began. One of these, which was current in the navy long after the event, was that one of the seamen on board the flagship, a Scillonian himself and with some experience of navigation, had judged that the ship was close to the Scillies. When he informed Sir Cloudesley of this, the admiral is purported to have had the man hanged for attempting to incite a mutiny! Robert Maybee (1810-1884) a poet from the islands, wrote the following lines about that event and the shipwreck which came after:

"Dark on the Gilston's rocky shore
  The mist came lowering down,
And night with all her deepening gloom
  Put on her sable crown.

From sea a wailing sound is heard,
  And the seamew's shrilly cry,
And booming surge and shrieking birds
  Proclaim strange danger nigh.

Wrong you steer, Sir Cloudesley, sure;
  The rocks of Scilly shun;
Northern move, or no sailor here
  Will see to-morrow's sun.

Hold, wretch! Dare tell your Admiral
  What dangers to evade?
I'll hang you up on yon yard-arm
  Before your prayers are said.

Oh, Admiral, before I die
  Let someone read aloud
The one hundred and ninth dread Psalm
  To all this sailor crowd.

Let it be done, cursed mutineer;
  As if I know not how
To steer my Association clear
  Of every danger now.

The Psalm was read, the wretch was hung;
  Drear darkness stalked around;
Whilst aloft the dead man swung,
  Three ships has struck the ground.

How sad and awful was the sight,
  How black and dark the shore.
Two thousand souls went down that night,
  And ne'er saw daylight more.

One man alone of that brave crew
  Was saved to tell the tale.
How swift and sure God's vengeance came;
  He can alone prevail."

Another story is that Sir Cloudesley was last seen floating on a raft with his pet dog. Perhaps the most famous of all the stories is one related by an old lady on her deathbed. She said that she found the admiral, with faint signs of life, on the beach, and that she killed him for the emerald ring he wore. Her confession was made to a clergyman who took the ring which finally passed into the hands of the Earl of Berkeley.

Cloudesley Shovell (there are several ways of spelling his first name) was born in 1650. His family may have had connections with Cockthorpe Hall. He was baptised in All Saints Church in the village of Cockthorpe in the same year. (A decade before that, John Narborough had been baptised in that same church. There cannot be too many churches in the land with the distinction of having had two future admirals christened in them.)

It appears that he started his sea career as a ship's boy, under the watchful eye of Narborough. In 1671, he was entered as a midshipman on the *Prince*, the flagship of James, Duke of York. On it, Shovell took part in the Battle of Sole Bay in 1672. It was fiercely fought, with an Anglo-French fleet opposing the Dutch under De Ruyter. The Dutch used fireships to such good effect that the honours went to them. The *Prince* was heavily damaged during the battle, and the Duke of York had to shift his flag no less than three times.

Later in that year, Shovell was one of over 200 volunteers entered on the *Fairfax*. He was appointed master's mate. In the following year when Narborough was appointed captain of the *St. Michael*, he took Shovell with him. When Narborough moved later into the *Henrietta*, Shovell appeared on the muster list as second lieutenant. The patronage of a senior officer was of considerable importance to a young man's career in those days, and indeed, that situation was to last in the navy until well into the present century.

In 1676 Lieut. Shovell was put in charge of the boats of the Mediterranean squadron, on a cutting-out and burning operation against the Tripoli pirates. It was a success, with four corsair galleys destroyed.

(With Shovell in this expedition was James Greeve of Cley-next-the-Sea. For his services, Greeve was given command of a captured ship called the *Orange Tree* of Algiers, and in the following year was presented with a gold medal by King Charles. Greeve died in 1686, and the facts outlined here can be read on the epitaph on his table-tomb in the churchyard of St. Margaret's at Cley.)

Shovell was appointed captain of the *Sapphire* by Narborough in 1677. This was followed by various other command appointments, always in the Mediterranean, until he returned to England in 1686. The records for this period of his service are sparse, but he appears to have conducted himself with some distinction.

He distinguished himself again at the Battle of Bantry Bay, although the English fleet came close to losing this battle fought in 1689. Fortunately the

Sir Cloudesley Shovell
(National Maritime Museum, London)

French admirals quarrelled amongst themselves, and failed to follow up their initial advantage. So the French, who were supporting the exiled James II, retreated. Shovell was knighted for his part in the battle.

In 1690 he was promoted to rear-admiral of the blue, and commanded a squadron in the Irish Sea. He played an important role in the Battle of Barfleur in 1692 where he broke the French line.

The quarrel between the Earl of Nottingham, Secretary of State, and Admiral Russell who commanded the fleet, in 1693, led to the appointment of a triumvirate of admirals to take over from Russell. Admirals Delaval, Killigrew, and Shovell, were selected. This retrograde step to a divided command, which had never been successful, fortunately did not last long. It is of interest to note that a Dutch cartoon of the period depicts Shovell with his hands tied behind his back, with the two ends of the cord being held by the other members of the trio. It possibly indicated the Dutch view of the relative professional abilities of the three.

Over the next few years he was involved in several more actions, but he found time in 1698 to be returned as MP for Rochester.

At the beginning of the War of the Spanish Succession in 1702, the Spanish decided to bring over from America a fleet of twenty great galleons carrying treasure. They crossed the Atlantic, met up with an escort of French warships, and sheltered in Vigo Bay. On the 12th October, Sir George Rooke in charge of a combined Anglo-Dutch fleet, crashed the boom there with his fireships and, after heavy fighting, won a brilliant victory. Admiral Shovell arrived a few days later, and was given the job of escorting the prizes and treasure back home. Unfortunately, in the process of leaving the bay, the largest of the treasure ships hit a small island and sank in 110 feet of water, and was lost. One imagines that Sir Cloudesley was not very popular with his colleagues after that.

In May 1703, he was commander-in-chief of the Mediterranean fleet. He had been ordered to renew treaties with the rulers of some of the Barbary States, and to try to persuade them to declare war on France. Shovell delegated this to Rear-Admiral George Byng. Byng was not able to persuade the Dey of Algiers to break with France, but was able to get previous treaties confirmed, and to get some additional protection for British and Colonial ships trading in the area. This episode highlights one of the important 'additional' duties of naval officers. They were often used in the field of diplomacy.

In the following year, in a fleet under the overall command of Admiral Rooke, Shovell took part in the capture of Gibraltar. In 1705, he captured Barcelona. He was returning from an unsuccessful attempt to capture Toulon in 1707, when he met his death on the Scillies.

In 1691 he had married Elizabeth, the widow of Sir John Narborough and had two daughters by her. The eldest of these, also called Elizabeth, married Sir Robert Marsham, Governor of Dover Castle, who was to be created Baron Romney in 1716. (This was the route by which some of Admiral Narborough's papers, including the log-book of the *Henry* mentioned in a previous section, entered the Romney library.)

Sir Cloudesley took his duties of step-father to the Narborough children very seriously. He helped advance the careers of the two boys in the navy. Unfortunately, they were on board the *Association* with him on that tragic night in 1707. Both were drowned. Lady Shovell managed to survive the shock of that triple tragedy, and died in 1732.

In the second bay of the south aisle of the nave of Westminster Abbey, there is a monument to Sir Cloudesley. It has been described as 'an extraordinary pompous celebration'. It consists of a sarcophagus on which reclines the figure of a man in Roman armour. The base is made up of panels carved with various trophies and a shipwreck. It is flanked with Corinthian columns which support entablatures and cherubs. The whole thing is of questionable taste, but Sir Cloudesley Shovell was not responsible for that.

Admiral of the Fleet George, Lord Anson (1697-1762) Oxnead and Ormesby Estates

George Anson is one of a handful of men who have been called the 'father of the Royal Navy'. His claim to that title is perhaps as good as most, but he is much better known for his voyage around the world, and for the great treasure he brought back from it. With part of his share of the treasure, Anson purchased the Paston estates in the Oxnead and Ormesby St. Margaret's area, after the Paston family fortunes had been squandered by the second Earl of Yarmouth.

Anson was born at Colwich, Staffordshire on the 23rd April 1697. Throughout his life he hated putting anything down on paper (his wife once expressed surprise when she received a letter from him), and in consequence little is known of his early career. He went to sea first when he was fourteen years old, and was commissioned a lieutenant in 1716.

He was a lieutenant on the *Montagu* in the action off Cape Passaro in 1718. In this action against the Spanish, 22 of their ships were either captured or sunk by the English fleet, despite the fact that war was not officially declared between the two nations until four months after the battle took place!

Anson was promoted to captain in 1723, and then had a long and fairly uneventful period on the American station, not returning to England until 1730. A Carolina lady writing home to her sister in England, said it was averred that he loved the bottle, and was far from being a woman-hater. It was said that he was handsome, polite and generous, was inclined to religion, and liked good music.

More uneventful years followed until 1737 when he was appointed to the *Centurion*, 60 guns. He was sent to guard the English traders on the West African coast, before being recalled in 1739. That year saw the start of the war against the Spanish called the 'War of Jenkin's Ear'. It was resolved to send a fleet against the Spanish settlements in the Caribbean, under Admiral 'Old Grog' Vernon, and as a subsidiary operation, to send a squadron into the Pacific to harass the Spanish there, and attempt to capture the annual treasure ship that sailed between Acapulco and Manila. Anson was placed in command of the Pacific squadron with the rank of commodore.

His six ships sailed in 1740. With the *Centurion* sailed the *Gloucester*, the *Severn*, the *Pearl*, the *Wager* and the *Tryall*. The ships were largely manned by pensioners from the Greenwich Hospital, and most of these were unfit even before the voyage started. The soldiers they carried from the Maritime Regiment were mostly untrained.

The only anti-scorbutic 'medicine' they carried was an entirely useless one called 'Dr. Ward's Drop and Pill'. It wasn't long before scurvy broke out amongst the crews. During the entire four year voyage only four men died from enemy action. 1,300 died from disease, mainly from scurvy. (The voyage left indelible scars on many of the survivors. Midshipman Augustus Keppel, later an admiral, always left his hat on and kept his mouth shut whenever in the future he sat for a portrait. He lost most of his hair and teeth during the *Centurion* voyage. Lieutenant Philip Saumarez, who as a captain in 1747 was cut down by a French cannonball at the age of only 34, would have died shortly anyway. A post-mortem revealed that his lungs had shrivelled to almost nothing from consumption contracted during this voyage.)

Two ships were wrecked on the South American coast, and one returned to England. The three survivors eventually made the appointed rendezvous at Juan Fernandez Island. After a period of rest and recuperation for the men, and after necessary repairs to the ships had been made, the *Centurion*, and her consorts *Gloucester* and *Tryall*, set out to raid Spanish settlements. Some booty was captured, but soon the *Tryall* had to be condemned, and her men were transferred to the remaining two ships. Later, the *Gloucester* too, was condemned and burnt.

In June 1743, off the Philippines, the *Centurion* met up with the Acapulco galleon, *Nuestra Senora de Covadonga*. and captured her. The ship carried a treasure estimated as having been worth about £800,000 (about £50m at today's valuation). When the ship arrived home in the following year, the treasure filled thirty-two wagons which were paraded through the City of London. Anson, as both commander-in-chief and captain, got three-eighths of its value. He had become exceedingly rich.

In 1745 he was promoted rear-admiral, and elevated again the following year. In May 1747, he led the fleet which off Finisterre captured an entire French squadron of 12 warships, and then took 6 merchantmen. The prize money rolled in.

He was raised to the peerage. In 1748 he married Lady Elizabeth Yorke, daughter of the Lord Chancellor. The few doors to power that might have been closed to him before, were now wide open.

From 1751 until his death in 1762, except for one short break, he was 1st Lord of the Board of Admiralty. He put in motion many changes in administrative processes. He improved training methods. He set about cutting out corruption and inefficiency in the naval dockyards. He established the Corps of Marines. He created a new code of the Articles of War. By the time he died, he had gone a long way to founding the naval profession, and creating the navy of Nelson. He did all this with scarcely any correspondence at all. (This is the main reason why no satisfactory biography of Anson has been written — the sources are so meagre.)

In his latter years he became rather austere and reserved. His prestige was such that he nearly always got his way, which did not make him popular in the political world. He cared not a fig for society, but he was popular in the navy. He died at Moor Park in Hertfordshire on the 6th June 1762.

Admiral George Townshend (1715-1769) Raynham

George Townshend was born in 1715, the eldest son of the second marriage (and therefore not in line for the title) of the second viscount. His uncle was Sir Robert Walpole.

He first went to sea at the age of 15, and about three years later was serving in the *Scarborough*. One of his shipmates on that vessel was Lieutenant Edward Hawke, who was to become one of England's greatest seamen.

George's career followed very much the standard pattern. At the age of 21, he passed his lieutenant's examination. Two years later he was promoted to captain. In the *Bedford* in 1744, he took part in the action off Toulon against the French and Spanish.

In this battle, the only British captain to distinguish himself out of the entire fleet of 29 ships, was Hawke on the *Berwick*. Admiral Thomas Mathews was in overall command, and the largely negative result of the action was in no small measure due to the friction, almost amounting to emnity, between Mathews and his second-in-command, Vice-Admiral Lestock. Later, both were court-martialled for neglect of duty. Mathews was condemned and dismissed the service.

In 1745 Townshend, still in the *Bedford*, was appointed commodore of a small squadron to operate on the Italian seaboard. He was given the duty of supporting Corsican insurgents against the French, and although he reduced the town of Bastia to ashes and destroyed two other forts, the French remained in control of most of Corsica. This was not Townshend's fault, for the Corsicans were given to fighting amongst themselves, and there was little he could do to bring the opposing factions together.

We come now to the controversial part of Townshend's career. In that same year he reported to his admiral, that, with only the *Bedford* and the *Essex* and two small bombs (ships mounted with mortars) at his disposal, he had sighted four large ships and two smaller ones that he took to be French men-of-war. He judged that the disproportion of forces was such as to preclude him seeking a battle. Townshend was court-martialled over the matter, and severely reprimanded, mainly it seems, for the fact that his reports were written *'with great carelessness and negligence'*.

He had various other commands after this, but it appears that he lost his only chance of glory in that incident off the coast of Corsica. He was made commander-in-chief of the Jamaica station, then in 1755, was promoted to rear-admiral of the white, and did further West Indian service. He returned to England in 1757, but did not go to sea again.

George Townshend was promoted to vice-admiral in 1758, and seven years later, to admiral. He died in August 1769.

The Townshend family have many other maritime connections. A namesake of the admiral, George, 4th Viscount and 1st Marquis Townshend (1724-1807), helped and befriended the young Thomas Manby whose father had been his aide-de-camp to the viscount in Ireland. The viscount's second wife, Anne, whom he married in 1773, was the patron of Edward Riou, who crops up several times in these pages due to his connections with Norfolk seamen. There is a pleasant little anecdote about Riou, which brings in Anne Townshend. It was related by Alexander Home, master's mate.

Riou was serving in Captain Cook's *Discovery* as a midshipman. The ship was at anchor in Queen Charlotte Sound, New Zealand in 1777. Young Neddy, as Riou was called, procured a native dog there, with the firm intention of bringing it home as a gift for his patroness. The dog was reputed to be cannibalistic and vicious, and had bitten several of Riou's shipmates. When he was ashore on duty, they killed, skinned, cooked and ate the dog. On Riou's return, the dog's skin was flung about his neck, much to his chagrin. He repaired below in a sulk. He brightened up only after he discovered that a prime portion of the cooked beast had been saved for him.

John, 4th Marquis Townshend (1798-1863) was also in the navy. He rose to be a rear-admiral. There is a memorial tablet to him in Raynham Church.

Rear-Admiral James Burney (1750-1821)
King's Lynn

James Burney's naval career had all the makings of a distinguished one, and then petered out. He is now better known for the 'Histories' he wrote than for his maritime achievements.

He was a member of the family which rated highly in the literary and artistic world of the 18th and 19th centuries. His father Charles, was a pupil of Dr. Arne, and studied the organ. James, his eldest son and second child, was born in London on the 13th June 1750. The family then moved to King's Lynn where Charles had been appointed organist to St. Margaret's Church. Two years to the day after James' birth, his sister Fanny was born. She was to write several novels and plays, and to become very famous indeed. Her 'Evelina' is still considered a classic, and in several ways presaged the works of Jane Austen. His brother Charles, the great scholar, was born in 1757.

James first went to sea at the age of ten, after spending some time at the Lynn Grammar School. He saw some action in the Seven Years War. His service in the navy was interrupted in 1770-1771, when he did a year on an East Indiaman called the *Greenwich*. He signed aboard Captain Cook's *Resolution* in 1771, where he was a shipmate of his fellow townsman George Vancouver. Burney passed his lieutenant's examination in 1772, and was made 2nd lieutenant of Cook's consort ship, the *Adventure*, later that same year at the Cape.

The ships parted company off New Zealand, and it was there that Burney was put in charge of the search party sent out to find a missing boat's crew under Midshipman Rowe. The 10 man crew of the boat had, in fact, been massacred. Burney was to write of the incident, *'We found no boat, but instead of her, such a shocking scene of carnage and barbarity as can never be mentioned or thought of but with horror; for the heads, hearts and lungs of several of our people were seen lying on the beach, and, at a distance, the dogs gnawing their intrails'*. It seems likely that but for Burney's skilful handling of the search, he and his crew might have had a similar end. The remains of the dead men were subsequently buried at sea.

Having failed to regain contact with the *Resolution*, Captain Tobias Furneaux decided to return home. They reached home in 1774, a year before the return of Cook.

Burney then joined the *Cerberus* on the North American station at a time when the colonies there were in revolt. He was recalled home in 1776, and at Cook's request joined the *Discovery* which was to sail with the *Resolution* on Cook's third, and last, voyage of exploration. He was 1st Lieutenant, and Vancouver was again a shipmate.

His journal of that voyage contains what is probably the fullest and most authoritative account of the death of Cook and the events that led up to it.

Back home in 1780, Burney was promoted to commander. He later saw service in several other ships. His sea service culminated in the years 1782-1784, when as captain of the *Bristol* of 50 guns, he served under Admiral Sir Edward

Hughes in Indian waters, and fought against the French Admiral Suffren. He was invalided home in 1784, and although he repeatedly offered his services thereafter to the Admiralty, they did not take him up. Exactly why the Admiralty overlooked the attributes of James Burney after 1784, we shall probably never know. It may have been the fact that he never hesitated to remind that august body of any defects he noted in the navy.

In 1785 he married Sally Payne. Between 1803 and 1817 he produced his five volume 'Chronological History of the Discoveries in the South Sea or Pacific Ocean', a work which within its own sphere is as important as his sister's novel is within its. He followed this with another work on the 'North-Eastern' discoveries. Amongst his other literary works was a book on the game of whist.

He was elected a Fellow of the Royal Society in 1809; the then President of the Society, the great Sir Joseph Banks, was a personal friend. He had many more friends in the literary world. They included Charles Lamb (who called him 'my friend the admiral'), Southey, and Hazlitt. He was described as being full of fun and good humour 'ever delighted of mirth in others'.

James Burney rose higher and higher on the seniority list of post-captains as his contemporaries died off, and was promoted to rear-admiral in the year of his death, 1821.

His name is perpetuated in the names of three places. Captain Cook named an island after him in the Bering Strait. Matthew Flinders, a friend and admirer, did the same in the Northern Territories of Australia. Cape Burney in Western Australia is also called after him.

John Fryer, Master RN. (1754-1817)
Wells-next-the-Sea

John Fryer's claim to fame is that he was master of the ship that was the centre of the most famous mutiny in maritime history. Fryer joined the *Bounty* on 20th August 1787, and probably rued that day a long time before the actual mutiny took place.

Fryer's record shows that he had been a master — the highest non-commissioned rank in the navy of his day — since 1781, when he had that appointment on *HMS Camel*. He was not to rise above that position during the whole of his service, although he certainly aspired to do so. His record on the *Bounty* shows him to have been both slow and indecisive, and probably petty-minded. It is possible that this last criticism could be levelled at most men, and not just Fryer, if they are cooped up on a small ship for months at a time, which creates a situation where small irritations grow quickly into large ones.

His relations with Captain Bligh, (we will call him that, although his substantive rank at that time was lieutenant), were good at first. Bligh wrote that he was *"a very good man and gives every satisfaction"*. Yet a few weeks later, he was to promote master's mate Fletcher Christian over Fryer's head into the postion of acting lieutenant. In doing so, Bligh made a lifelong enemy in Fryer.

This emnity was to show itself on several occasions. Probably the most serious of these occured after Fryer had already given Bligh ample reason to revise his previous estimation of the master's worth. Fryer was asked to countersign some official documents, and at first he refused to do so unless Bligh guaranteed him a good letter of recommendation at the end of the voyage. This was tantamount to mutiny, and Fryer quickly changed his mind when Bligh assembled the crew and read out the Articles of War.

Fryer was later involved in running the ship ashore in Tahiti, and also let one of the chronometers run down. He consorted with one of the local ladies there, (as did everyone else with the exception of Bligh himself), and created a fracas with the natives when he refused to return some of her property. For this, he was on the receiving end of Bligh's temper again.

As master, Fryer was responsible for looking after the keys to the armourer's chests which held the ship's small arms. After the ship left Tahiti, Fryer made an unauthorised arrangement with the armourer, that he, the armourer, should hold on to the keys. As it turned out, this arrangement helped Christian to arm his men at the time of the mutiny.

Fryer was arrested by the mutineers along with his captain. Together with 17 other men, the two were sent down into the ship's boat. It is on record that Fryer asked to stay with the ship, but this does not mean that he wished to join the mutineers. The boat the loyalists were placed in was only 23 feet long, less than 7 feet wide, and when they were all aboard, had a freeboard of only 7 inches. It was probably that which made Fryer wish to stay with the *Bounty*! Several of the men who did stay on board were not mutineers either.

The subsequent boat voyage, an epic feat that was to last 43 days and take them 3618 miles to Timor (an open boat journey which was not surpassed until World War II), created more tension between Fryer and his captain. Bligh several times took Fryer to task, on one occasion for starting a fire on an island on which the men were attempting to stay hidden from hostile natives. The pair even had an argument about the recipe for oyster stew! At Timor, they reached the nadir of their relationship, and communicated with each other only in writing.

After they arrived back home in England, the antipathy continued. Bligh refused a request from Captain Edward Riou for a character reference for Fryer. In his turn, Fryer aided Edward Christian, Fletcher's brother, in that man's efforts to blacken Bligh's character and save his brother's.

There can be no doubt that John Fryer was but an average non-commissioned officer, one of the type of which the navy of that time must have had many. However, both before and after the *Bounty* voyage, Fryer's conduct was always reported on as good, if not exemplary. So perhaps the incompetence he showed under Bligh was brought about by the dislike the men developed for each other. Bligh was not the ogre — the character portrayed by Charles Laughton — we have all come to hate, (and Fletcher Christian was far from being the character portrayed by Clark Gable we have all come to admire). Bligh was an excellent navigator (as befits one who had sailed under Captain Cook); he was courageous, and was a redoubtable fighter (this was noted by no better judge of men than Nelson himself, at the Battle of Copenhagen). He was, however, coarse-mouthed, bad-tempered, and lacked knowledge of what we now call man-management. He was not a cruel man — there were comparatively few floggings on the *Bounty*. To Fryer must go a share of the blame for the undeserved reputation for cruelty and oppression that has been built up around Bligh's name since the *Bounty* incident. Only in recent years have there been major attempts to 'rehabilitate' him.

Like Bligh, Fryer too was at the Battle of Copenhagen, but not of course on the same ship.

Fryer died in 1817, and was buried in the churchyard of St. Nicholas at Wells-next-the-Sea, where he had been baptised sixty-three years previously. Unfortunately, no record was kept of the position of his grave when the tombstones there were removed. Vice-Admiral of the Blue William Bligh, F.R.S., sometime Governor of the colony at Botany Bay, died in that same year. He too, was sixty-three years old.

Why did the mutiny on the *Bounty* take place? There has been more written about this matter than perhaps any other incident in maritime history. The theories are legion. One historian has even claimed that Bligh and Christian were a pair of lovers who had fallen out with each other!

The mutiny was not caused by Bligh's cruelty, for he was not a cruel man. Some of the less attractive facets of his character, may have been contributory factors, but that is all. Later in his career he was involved in two other mutinies, and in those he was nearly blameless as well. At the mutiny at the Nore in 1797, his was only one of many ships involved. When he was Governor of New South Wales he attempted, quite correctly, to curb the excesses of the local militia officers engaged in the rum trade. They rebelled.

The basic cause of the *Bounty* mutiny is probably a simple one. The crew had experienced a long hard voyage to Tahiti. Then they had about six months stay in what for most of them must have seemed like heaven on earth, while they collected the bread-fruit specimens they were to transport to the West Indies. This was a far longer stay than any previous European ship had made. Now they had before them the long voyage to the West Indies, and they must all have made mental comparisons between their idyllic days on the island, where food and the favours of ladies were plentiful, and the deprivations they could expect on the voyage ahead. It is small wonder they mutinied.

Norfolk has one other connection with one of the major participants in the mutiny, although it is a rather tenuous and tortuous one. Fletcher Christian's uncle Humphrey Christian (1720-1773) came to Norfolk and married Elizabeth Brett of Docking. Their son inherited Docking Hall. One of the conditions of the inheritance was that he had to change his name to Hare.

David Bartleman, Master (1756-1781)
Great Yarmouth

Just as the lonely stretches of the Norfolk coastline have always attracted the attentions of smugglers, the busy sea routes adjacent to that coast have always been a happy hunting ground for wreckers and pirates. There is a record from the 14th century of an Italian ship which foundered off Blakeney with 'help' from wreckers. The men involved in the wrecking operation then helped to save the lives of the merchants and seamen on board, and in the process made off with most of the ship's cargo. These widespread practices didn't end with the Middle Ages.

In the churchyard of St. Nicholas, Great Yarmouth, there is a headstone which for sheer verbosity (if a piece of stone covered in words can be so described), rivals most. Carved on it is a full and exciting description of a piratical incident that took place off Yarmouth as late as 1781. It reads:

To
The Memory of
DAVID BARTLEMAN
Master of the Brig Alexander & Margaret
Of North Shields
Who on the 31st Jan 1781 on the Norfolk Coast
With only three 8 pounders and ten Men and Boys
Nobly defended himself
Against a Cutter carrying eighteen 4 pounders
And upwards of a Hundred Men
Commanded by the notorious English Pirate
FALL
and fairly beat him off
Two hours after the Enemy came down upon him again
When totally disabled his Mate Daniel MacAuley
Expiring with the loss of blood
And himself dangerously wounded
He was obliged to strike and ransome
He brought his shattered Vessel into Yarmouth
With more
Than the Honours of a Conqueror
And died here in consequence of his wounds
On the 14th February following
In the 25th Year of his Age
To commemorate the Gallantry of his Son
The Bravery of his faithful Mate
And at the same time Mark the Infamy of a
Savage Pirate
His afflicted Father ALEXANDER BARTLEMAN
Has ordered this Stone to be erected over his
Honourable Grave

The carving doesn't end there. There is a blessing underneath. One must hope that the infamous Fall ended up with his just deserts.

Captain George Vancouver (1757-1798) King's Lynn

On the 30th January 1774, Captain Cook's ship *Resolution* reached the latitude 71 degrees 10 minutes, the farthest south recorded by any ship up to that time. (Cook had been searching for the imaginary Southern Continent.) The ship was now faced with a barrier of ice which prevented further southward movement, so she was brought about. Young George Vancouver climbed out to the end of the bowsprit just before this process was begun, and thus claimed to have been nearer the South Pole than any other man. Sixteen year old Vancouver was showing the spirit of adventure that was never to leave him, and the incident gave him a story on which he was to dine out many times in later years.

He had joined the *Resolution* at Deptford in January 1772, at the start of Cook's second voyage around the world. What influence his family were able to bring to bear to get him one of the coveted posts on the ship is not known. It must however, have carried considerable weight, as after the success of Cook's first voyage, and the known excellence of the training received by his young officers, rivalry for the vacant positions must have been intense. It is possible that the position held by George's father, John Jasper Vancouver, had something to do with it. Vancouver the elder was deputy-customer at King's Lynn, the senior executive position in the Custom's service for the district. The family were of Dutch origin on John Jasper's side. He married Bridget Berners at All Saint's Church, King's Lynn, in 1749. The Berners were an old East Anglian family who could trace their ancestry back to Sir Richard Grenville of the *Revenge*.

George was born on 22nd June 1757 in the family residence in the town. He was the sixth and youngest child in the family.

Vancouver's journal — all officers were obliged to keep one — of this first voyage of his, has disappeared. In consequence, we know little about his activities during the three-and-a-half years he was away. Cook must have had a good opinion of him, however, for George was appointed to the *Discovery* on that great navigator's third and final voyage. Vancouver's journal for this voyage too, has vanished, so the only records we have of him are references in the journals of others.

He was involved in the build-up of events which led to Cook's death, although he was not in the particular fight concerned. Thomas Edgar, master of the *Discovery*, wrote in his journal that in one fracas with the Sandwich Islanders, Vancouver stepped between a weapon-wielding native and Edgar, and took a blow meant for the master. Later, Vancouver was involved in the efforts to recover the remains of Cook.

The *Resolution* and *Discovery* arrived back in the Thames in 1780. In that same year, Vancouver passed his examination for lieutenant. He subsequently saw service in the Caribbean. He carried out surveys of Port Royal and Kingston Harbours. The resulting chart was of very high standard, as befits one who had served under Cook.

Vancouver had only one lengthy period on half-pay, and that was in

1783-1784. In 1789, he was appointed to be second in command of an expedition to the South Seas which was later called off. In the following year, he was appointed to command an expedition to the North West Pacific.

His orders were to look for the western end of the North West Passage, and officially to receive back from the Spanish certain British property seized by them in 1789 at Nootka Sound, on what is now called Vancouver Island. (The Nootka Sound incident had almost resulted in war between Britain and Spain.)

On 1st April 1791, his two ships, the *Discovery* and the *Chatham*, sailed from the Thames. Later, they were to meet up with the *Daedalus*, storeship. Several other Norfolk men sailed on these ships. Two of them, Spelman Swaine of King's Lynn, and Thomas Manby of Hilgay, were later to rise to the rank of rear-admiral. John Langley, marine, ended up as an innkeeper at Lynn.

The ships sailed via the Cape of Good Hope. At the Cape, the Dutch rather fêted Vancouver, as a prôtége of Cook. They then sailed for New Holland. They approached that coast with some considerable care, *'not choosing to make too free with a coast entirely unexplored'*, Vancouver wrote. They landed at King George Sound, and conducted a survey there. They next stopped at New Zealand, before proceeding to Tahiti.

Vancouver was well received there. Two chiefs survived from the time of Cook's last visit, and remembered him. It was here that Vancouver made several decisions that were extremely unpopular with his crews. When he made them, he probably had the fate of the *Bounty* in mind. (Bligh had reached home after the mutiny, twelve months before Vancouver sailed). He forbade all shore leave, and banned all private trading until the ship's stocks had been replenished. It was here at Tahiti that obvious signs of his failing health started to show themselves. He lost his temper at the slightest provocation, and violently reacted to the theft of some shirts.

Vancouver was a stern disciplinarian, and there is more than a little evidence in the journals of some of his officers, that he was not too popular with them. Like his mentor Cook, he often kept his own counsel and kept his officers in the dark. His treatment of midshipmen was harsh, and several refused invitations to dine with him. One midshipman he had flogged, not once, but three times. Flogging of a junior officer was not unusual in the navy of the day, but in this case there were special circumstances, and Vancouver must later have often regretted ordering these floggings carried out.

The midshipman concerned was Thomas Pitt, a man with very high connections, for he was cousin to Prime Minister William Pitt. He was of very unstable character. In 1789, he had somehow earned the ire of another of Cook's young gentlemen, Capt. Edward Riou, who subsequently refused to give Pitt a recommendation. In later life, he killed a fellow officer in a duel, before being killed in one himself. We don't know all the details of the events which led to the floggings, but certainly two or three of his shipmates thought that the punishments were harsh. As we shall see later, Pitt was to get his revenge of sorts.

When the ships arrived at Nootka Sound Vancouver accomplished his diplomatic tasks with the Spanish with a high degree of skill and tact. The fact

George Vancouver
(National Portrait Gallery, London; there is some doubt of the authenticity of this portrait)

that this area finally became British Columbia is directly attributable to his actions.

Vancouver now set about looking for the North West Passage, and charting the area. He did not find the passage, but his search resulted in one of the most brilliant hydrographic surveys ever conducted. He had chronometers aboard which enabled him to find his position with some accuracy. He also had aboard copies of the journals of Nathaniel Portlock and George Dixon (both of whom had also sailed with Cook), who had visited this coast on a trading voyage made between 1785 and 1788. The charts he and his officers produced were so good that some of them were still in use into the present century.

The coast of north-western America is an especially difficult one both to navigate and to chart. There are innumerable islands and rocks and the channels are narrow and perilous to shipping even in these days. There are treacherous currents, tide-rips, and swirling eddies. None of these difficulties put off George Vancouver. He kept to his task, like the professional and perfectionist he was.

He commemorated his family and many of the places connected with them, in the names he gave to the places he discovered and explored. The map of the coast of north-west Canada is covered in names with Norfolk connections. There is a Lynn Channel, a Holkham Bay, a Port Snettisham, and a Port Houghton. There is a Point Coke (after Thomas Coke), and a Point Windham (after the Norfolk statesman William Windham). His mother's birthplace, St. Mary Wiggenhall, is commemorated at Point St. Marys, and her maiden name at Berner's Bay. Part of Alaska he named New Norfolk, but this has not survived.

It is of interest to note that the Seymour Narrows, which Vancouver was the first to explore, are still considered very difficult and dangerous to navigation, even after the blasting away of the double peaks of the Ripple Rock in 1958.

Vancouver returned home with his ships in 1795, with his health destroyed. As happened all too frequently amongst the ranks of seamen-explorers, the hard conditions under which they lived and worked took their toll. He did not go to sea again, and spent his last years in preparing his journals and charts for publication. His health deteriorated steadily, and his life was made exceedingly uncomfortable by the actions and machinations of the revenge seeking Thomas Pitt, now Lord Camelford. Camelford challenged Vancouver to a duel, although the Admiralty stepped in to have the challenge withdrawn, and attacked him physically in a London street. The incident became the subject of a cartoon by Gillray, and gained some notoriety as a result. Camelford was probably also behind the spreading of unfounded rumours that there had been a mutiny on the *Discovery*.

George Vancouver died, probably of myxodema, on the 12th May 1798. He had not married. He was buried at Petersham. He died with the editing of his journals uncompleted. The work was finished by his brother John, and was published under the title, "A Voyage of Discovery to the North Pacific Ocean and Round the World". It is a fitting memorial to one who was probably the most able of Cook's 'young gentlemen'.

Sadly, Vancouver's birthplace has been pulled down. The site is now occupied by the China Garden Restaurant in the bustling modern shopping precinct of King's Lynn, called the Vancouver Centre.

Earlier in this century it was written, "Vancouver is undoubtedly the worst documented of all famous 18th century navigators. He did his work. He died. He was forgotten". Thankfully, that is no longer true. Although perhaps still remembered more in Canada, where a statue of him sits atop the Parliament Building, Victoria, than in his native country, a major re-assessment of his work has taken place over the past few years. He now stands where he should have always been, firmly amongst that most select band of explorer-navigators.

Vice-Admiral Horatio, Viscount Nelson (1758-1805)
Burnham Thorpe

In the 31st year of the reign of George II, two isolated events took place in England. Horatio Nelson, who was to become the greatest fighting sailor that any country has produced, was born on the 29th September 1758. In that same year, the Admiralty placed an order with the Chatham Dockyard for a ship that, when launched in 1765, was to be named the *Victory*. Nelson's association with that ship was to become as famous as that of Drake and the *Golden Hind*, and of Columbus and the *Santa Maria*.

Nelson was born at the Rectory at Burnham Thorpe, where his father Edmund Nelson was the incumbent. Horatio was the sixth of eleven children, and was at first so weak and puny that he was not expected to live. He survived to take up one of the most arduous of all careers, a life at sea. His health was to be a problem for him all his life, quite apart from the horrific injuries he was to sustain.

When fully grown, he was less than five feet six inches tall, and was described as being slender to thin. In common with a lot of his contemporaries, he had chronic sinus trouble which made his speech slightly nasal. His speech was also coloured with the Norfolk accent, which he never lost.

At the age of 9, he became a pupil at the Norwich Grammar School. This was followed by a period at Downham Market School, where one of his fellow pupils was George Manby, who was to become famous as the inventor of the rocket life-saving apparatus. It was probably Manby who wrote many years later in an unsigned magazine article, that it was Nelson's "*pleasure to set small boys working the pump in the village street, so that he could sail paper boats in the resulting stream*". (It should be noted that some authorities dispute the Nelson-Manby connection, played upon often by Manby in his later years, because of the disparity in their ages. Manby was seven years younger than Nelson, and would have been only 3, when Nelson was at Downham.)

Nelson's third school was the Paston Grammar School at North Walsham. One of the 'houses' there is named after him.

Nelson's mother died when he was only 9 years old. His eldest sister Susannah married a merchant from Wells-next-the-Sea named Thomas Bolton. That couple made their home in Burnham Market, and their residence there, Bolton House, still stands. Nelson's birthplace has long since been demolished, but there is a plaque commemorating the event on a wall near to the site where the house once stood.

Through the offices of his uncle Captain Maurice Suckling, who was commander of the ship, Nelson was appointed midshipman aboard the *Raisonnable* in 1771. He was then 12½ years old. He saw no active service on this ship, and it was the same story when he followed his uncle into the *Triumph*. She was a guardship moored in the Thames.

Nelson then did a year in the Merchant Service on a voyage to the West Indies. It was a valuable year. It gave him an appreciation of the value of that

Service and of its men, an outlook not shared by every naval officer of the day. Nelson wrote of this voyage, '*if I did not improve my education, I came back a practical seaman, with a horror of the Royal Navy*'. (This horror was probably caused by the activities of the Press Gang — or Impress Service, as it should be called.)

In 1773 Nelson joined the *Carcass* on a scientific expedition to the Arctic. It was on this voyage that he and a shipmate had the famous encounter with a bear on the ice. They were endeavouring to shoot the bear, the gun misfired, and Nelson wanted to have a go at the animal with the musket's butt-end. The animal was scared off by a gun fired from the ship. The captain of the *Carcass*, afterwards Admiral Lutwidge, often used to tell this story after his young charge had become famous.

Nelson next saw service in Indian waters, but was invalided home when he went down with fever. He passed his lieutenant's examination in 1777, and then joined the frigate *Lowestoffe* bound for the West Indies.

The American colonies were now in revolt, and they were aided by French privateers, so there was plenty of action to be seen. Nelson impressed his superiors with his diligence, initiative, and his courage. He was promoted to commander in 1778, and took charge of a brig called the *Badger*. He was in the thick of things again, and so distinguished himself, that in June of the following year whilst still only 20 years old, he was promoted to post-captain. This was an important step, for from that rank upwards promotion was made strictly on order of seniority, and so the earlier one got on the ladder, the better. He was given command of the *Hinchinbrooke*, and then of the *Janus*. However, he again contracted fever and was invalided home once more.

In the following year he was given the frigate *Albemarle*, and served in the Baltic and on the North American station. In 1782, at Quebec, he experienced the first of his several love affairs. He saw little in the way of other action, and when the American War of Independence came to an end, the entire fleet was ordered home.

In 1784 he was back in the West Indies with the *Boreas*. Two years later on the island of Nevis, he met Frances Nisbet, a young widow with a five year old son. He married her in 1787, and both returned to England.

Nelson then experienced the most frustrating period of his life. He was ashore for five years on 'half-pay', a euphemism (with the appropriate monetary penalty) for being out of work. In 1793 he was rescued from his inactivity when war with France broke out once more. He was given the *Agamemnon* of 64 guns, and this turned out to be his favourite ship. Many of his crew were from Norfolk, having answered his call for volunteers. One of these was Tom Allen, born at Burnham Thorpe in 1764, who joined as Nelson's body-servant.

The *Agamemnon* joined the Mediterranean fleet under Lord Hood. The previous five years inactivity were to be made up for, and he soon earned the reputation of being the most active of Hood's captains. Wherever the action was, Nelson seemed to be. At the siege of Calvi, he received the wound that blinded his right eye.

In several engagements with the enemy he rendered distinguished service.

In consequence, in 1795, he was made an Honorary Colonel of the Marines, and the extra salary that went with the sinecure was gratefully received, for he was never very well off. (One of the two other captains to be granted this honour on the same occasion, was the Hon. George Berkeley about whom we shall have more to say in an anecdote at the end of this section.)

Nelson was promoted to commodore in 1796, and hoisted his flag in the *Captain*. On this ship he fought at the Battle of St. Vincent on the 14th February 1797. In this battle, the British fleet under Jervis won a resounding victory against a Spanish fleet twice its size. This victory was in no small measure due to Nelson's initiative in leaving the line of battle (normally a court-martial offence, but nothing succeeds like success!) to block off the Spaniard's retreat. It was during this process that Nelson performed the feat of boarding and capturing one Spanish vessel, and then using that as a bridge, boarding and capturing another. British tars loved daring deeds, and they especially loved this one. There was to be no court-martial for Nelson; he was knighted for his part in the battle. In addition his promotion to rear-admiral came through.

In the following year, in command of a small force and flying his flag in the *Theseus*, in an attempt to capture a Spanish treasure ship at Tenerife, he was wounded in the right arm which had to be amputated.

After a long period of convalescence, Nelson joined Admiral Jervis (now Lord St. Vincent) at Cadiz. He was now on board the *Vanguard*. Jervis sent him — a stroke of genius as it turned out — with an independent fleet into the Mediterranean with orders to seek out the French Toulon fleet. On August 1st 1798, Nelson found the French at Aboukir Bay near one of the mouths of the Nile. In a night action, eleven of the thirteen French ships-of-the-line were either captured or destroyed. Nelson was slightly wounded in the battle.

After the Battle of the Nile, Nelson proceeded to the Bay of Naples. Many honours were showered upon him, and he was raised to the peerage. He renewed his acquaintance (they had first met in 1793) with Emma, Lady Hamilton, and their love affair, that was to shock the nation and shake the naval establishment, started in earnest.

The effect on the Establishment back home can best be illustrated by quoting from a Biographical Dictionary published in 1838. First, on Emma it said:

> *'At 16, she went to London, and after various adventures in low life, she was reduced to the greatest distress. From this state she was relieved by the infamous Dr. Graham, who took her to his house, and there exhibited her, covered in a transparent veil . . .'*

The same book, in its section on Nelson, has this to say:

> *'And here we are compelled to record the fact that during the admiral's stay at Naples, he fell under the fascination of Lady Hamilton, the wife of the English Ambassador; allowed her to exercise a most pernicious influence over him; that he lived publically with her after the death of her husband; and as a natural consequence, that it produced a separation between him and Lady Nelson on his return.'*

Nelson wounded off Tenerife
(From a print by R. A. Westhall)

In addition to becoming embroiled with Emma, Nelson also got himself involved in the affairs of the independent state of Naples. He was even involved in the judicial murder of a Jacobin rebel called Commodore Caracciolo, an act, probably the only despicable one of his career, for which he was afterwards severely criticised. He was recalled home. He was a hero, but a somewhat tarnished one, and the Admiralty quickly sent him to the Baltic as second-in-command of a fleet under Admiral Sir Hyde Parker.

The Battle of Copenhagen was fought on 2nd April 1801. The battle commenced with Parker holding off to the north, Nelson giving battle in the south, and with Rear-Admiral Graves, also engaging the enemy, between the two. Captain Edward Riou in the *Amazon* was placed in charge of a squadron of frigates and smaller ships, with orders from Nelson to act as circumstances might require.

It was an extremely hard fought battle. British losses were high. Three ships-of-the-line had run ashore, and Riou, seeing this, took his small ships in to fill the gap in the British line. He commenced bombarding the powerful Trekonis Fort, which was to have been the target for the missing and more powerful ships. Riou had thus placed himself between Parker and Graves.

In the thick of the battle, Parker signalled for action to cease, and the famous incident of Nelson aboard the *Elephant*, putting his telescope to his blind eye occured. Nelson kept his 'engage the enemy' signal flying. Admiral Graves, caught between his two superiors, copied Parker's signal on the side where Nelson couldn't see it, and Nelson's on the side where it was not visible to Parker, and carried on fighting with his ship, the *Defiance*. Poor Riou, positioned as he was between Parker and Graves, had no option but to cease firing. He is reported to have said, 'What will Nelson think of us?' As the *Amazon* turned away, a cannon shot from the fort cut the already wounded Riou in two.

Gradually, Danish resistance lessened. Their flagship blew up, and finally a ceasefire was agreed. Nelson's tenacity and the courage of those under him, had won the day.

(Nelson could have done with the services of *HMS Invincible* of 74 guns, during this battle. Unfortunately, on the 16th March, as she was hastening to join the fleet, she went ashore on Hammonds Knoll off Happisburgh on the Norfolk coast. Out of the crew of 550, 400 men were lost. 119 of them lie in an unmarked grave in a corner of the Happisburgh churchyard.)

After the battle, Nelson singled out one of his captains for special honour, and was to write a note-worthy commendation about another. He called Captain William Bligh (once of the *Bounty*) of the *Glatton*, to the flagship, and publicly thanked him for his support. Later, Nelson wrote, '*If it had not been for the untoward accident of three of our line getting on shore ... my plan would have been complete ... In that case, poor dear Riou might have been saved; and his bravery attempted what I directed three sail of the line to assist him in*'. It is of interest to note that the two officers concerned, Bligh and Riou, had earlier been shipmates under Captain Cook.

In the same year as Copenhagen, Nelson was made an Honorary Member of the Levant Company, a company his fellow Norfolkman John Eldred had helped to set up many years before.

In 1803 Viscount Nelson as he now was, was given command of the Mediterranean fleet, with his flag aboard the *Victory*. So the two comparatively minor events that occured in 1758 came together, in a combination of man and ship now known the world over.

For the next two years Nelson was preoccupied with trying to prevent the French fleet under Villeneuve joining up with other French and Spanish units. At one time he chased the French across the Atlantic.

The fleets finally met off Trafalgar on 21st October 1805. It ended with victory for the British who did not lose a single ship. The French and Spanish lost eighteen, with over 6,000 men killed or wounded. Nelson had won the battle, but at the cost of his own life. Before the fighting began he had flown his 'England expects' signal, and during it had worn his full uniform with decorations, making him an obvious target for enemy marksmen. His last words were, 'Thank God I have done my duty'. Nelson had attained the glory that he had spent his life seeking.

Nelson was a born leader of men. He was ever able to get the best out of his people by always being prepared to lead from the front. He could be a stern disciplinarian but that did not prevent his men loving him. On one of his ships, with a crew of only 190, he had once ordered a total of 49 floggings in a year. When Earl St. Vincent's decision to hang four guilty mutineers on the Sabbath caused something of a furore in the fleet, Nelson backed his superior, and said that in the same circumstances he would have hung them had it been Christmas Day. Even so, his character was such that on leaving the *Foudroyant* in 1800, the men of his barge crew could send him the following letter:

> *'My Lord, It is with extreme grief that we find you are about to leave us. We have been along with you (though not in the same ship) in every engagement your Lordship has been in, both by sea and land; and must humbly beg of your Lordship to permit us to go to England, as your boats crew, in any ship or vessel, or in any way that may seem most pleasing to your Lordship. My Lord, pardon the rude style of seamen, who are but little acquainted with writing, and believe us to be, my Lord, your ever humble and obedient servants.'*

After Nelson was killed a seaman named Sam on the *Royal Sovereign*, who himself had lost three fingers of his left hand during the battle, wrote a letter home to his father. Part of it reads:

> *'Our dear Admiral Nelson is killed! So we have paid pretty sharply for licking 'em. I never sat eyes on him, for which I am both sorry and glad; for, to be sure, I should have liked to have seen him — but then, all the men in our ship who have seen him are such soft toads, they have done nothing but blast their eyes, and cry, ever since he was killed. God bless you! Chaps that fought like the devil, sit down and cry like a wench. I am still in the Royal*

Sovereign, but the Admiral (Collingwood) has left her, for she is like a horse without a bridle, so he is in a frigate that he may be here and there and everywhere, for he's as cute as here and there one, and as bold as a lion, for all he can cry! — I saw his tears with my own eyes, when the boat hailed and said my lord was dead. So no more at present from your dutiful son'.

Soon after the Battle of the Nile, one of Nelson's captains, Benjamin Hallowell, had got his ship's carpenter to make a coffin from the mast of one of the battered French ships, the *L'Orient*. He presented this coffin to Nelson with a note to the effect that he wished the admiral might be buried in it but at a time in the far future. Nelson carried that coffin with him on several voyages, and was quite proud of it. He was buried in it on the 9th January 1806 in St. Paul's Cathedral.

Nelson's title passed to his elder brother William, (an undeserving character with none of his brother's attributes), who was also created Earl Nelson of Trafalgar. When William died, the titles devolved upon Thomas, the son of Susannah and Thomas Bolton.

Emma Hamilton, who was not looked after by a 'grateful nation' in accordance with Nelson's wishes, died in penury at Calais on the 15th January 1815. Her daughter by Nelson, Horatia, married Philip Ward the curate of Burnham Westgate Church in 1823.

Tom Allen, Nelson's long-serving body servant, was taken on in the same capacity by Captain Sir William Bolton. Sir William had married Susannah's daughter Kate — his own cousin. When Bolton died, Tom Allen was appointed 'Pewterer' to Greenwich Hospital, through the good offices of the then Governor, Nelson's friend and one-time flag-captain, Sir Thomas Hardy (by then a rear-admiral). Allen died there in 1838.

There are many portraits of Nelson, and not a few paintings of episodes from his career. Several in the latter genre were painted by Richard Westhall RA. According to 'White's Norfolk' of 1845, Westhall was born at Reepham in the county, in 1765. Westhall also painted at least two pictures of Emma Hamilton. His younger step-brother, William, also had 'maritime connections'. He was the official artist to Captain Matthew Flinder's voyage of exploration to Australia, on the *Investigator* which sailed from England in 1801.

There are not too many humorous stories about the infamous (albeit necessary) Press Gangs, and as this one has a slight Nelsonian connection, it is perhaps worth relating here. It concerns Admiral the Hon. Sir George Berkeley who as a captain had been given an honorary title in the marines at the same time as Nelson. This anecdote used to be told by the Duke of Wellington at breakfast parties he held in the 1830's.

The Admiral was commanding the fleet at Lisbon during the Peninsular War. While living ashore there he became decidedly annoyed by a Minorcan painter, a miniaturist, who had fallen desperately in love with his daughter, Mary Caroline. The painter wrote her several letters announcing his passion. At last, on his bringing one of these in person to the admiral's door, the admiral desired him to be taken to the police. The Minorcan argued strongly against this procedure, declaring that he was a British subject. It was indeed found upon investigation that he had been born in Minorca when it was still under British dominion. "Oh! then," said the admiral, "if you are a British subject, well and good. Send for a sergeant of the marines!" He had the painter pressed and sent aboard his flagship, the *Harfleur*. There the Minorcan remained, and was set to paint the ship, alternately painting and being flogged, until finally someone interceded for him and he was freed. (The admiral's daughter married Henry, the Earl of Euston in 1812. She became the Duchess of Grafton when her husband succeeded to that title in 1844. The seat of the Duke was at Euston Hall, near Thetford.)

Rear-Admiral Sir Edward Berry (1768-1831)
Catton

Of all the captain's in Nelson's select 'Band of Brothers', it is likely that Edward Berry was one of the admiral's favourites. After the Battle of St. Vincent, Nelson was to write, *'The first man who jumped into the enemy's mizzen chains was Captain Berry'*. Later, when he took Berry along to court with him, and the king commented upon the loss of his right arm, Nelson promptly presented Berry as his right hand.

Berry was Nelson's flag-captain at the Battle of the Nile, and when Nelson was wounded there, it was into Berry's arms that he fell. In 1805, the *Amagemnon* with Berry in command arrived only just in time to take part in the Battle of Trafalgar. When the *Agamemnon* was sighted from the deck of the *Victory*, it is reported that his lordship rubbed his hands together and said, 'Now we'll have a fight!'

After he finished his active service in the navy, Edward Berry lived in a house called 'The Warren' at Catton, now a suburb of Norwich. He lived there from 1814 until 1822, when ill-health made him take up residence at Bath, where he died in 1831.

It was said of Berry, that with the exception of Collingwood, no one in the navy of his time had seen so much action. Except for the Battle of Copenhagen he had taken part in just about every major engagement there had been.

He was made a baronet in 1806, and a KCB in 1815. He had married his first cousin Louisa, daughter of the Reverend Dr. Forster of Norwich, in 1797, after being exhorted by Nelson to get the matter over with quickly. Nelson wrote, *'If you mean to marry, I would recommend your doing it speedily, or the to-be Mrs. Berry will have very little of your company . . .'*. This was just prior to his appointment as Nelson's flag-captain on the *Vanguard*. The couple did not have any children, and in consequence the baronetcy became extinct on Berry's death.

Vice-Admiral William Lukin (1768-1833)
Felbrigg

William Lukin, who was later to inherit the Felbrigg estates and change his name to Windham, was born in 1768. He was the son of the Rev. George William Lukin, sometime Dean of Wells, who was a grandson of William Windham (1674-1730).

Like most young men who took up a sea-going life at that time, he joined his first ship at an early age. He was a lieutenant at 25, and two years later was given command of a sloop. He was made post-captain in that same year.

In the spring of 1797, there occured the mutiny of the Channel Fleet at Spithead. This resulted from the culmination of a number of long-standing grievances, and if ever a mutiny can be said to be justified, then this one could. The men were complaining about poor pay (often months and even years in arrears), poor food and not enough of it, and other harsh conditions of service. It was organised by men in the *Queen Charlotte*, but was supported by crews throughout the fleet. One of these was the *Thames*, Captain Lukin commanding.

For the most part, the mutineers acted with moderation. As England was involved in the Revolutionary War with France, the men knew that time was on their side, and they stood firm as senior admiral after senior admiral attempted to restore obedience. Finally, the men's requests were acceded to, together with a full pardon for all involved from the king. Unfortunately, the matter didn't end there, for in May of the same year, mutiny also broke out at the Nore. That one did not end so amicably.

Captain Lukin gained credit for the fact that the *Thames* was the first vessel to put to sea from Spithead after the suppression of the mutiny there. This was more of an achievement than appears at first sight, in view of the vessel's destination. She was to join the West Indies station, and that was by far the least liked of all naval areas of duty, due to the diseases that were always rampant out there and the resulting relatively high death rate.

One of Lukin's last ships was the *Mars* of 74 guns. In this ship he was part of a small squadron under the overall command of Sir Samuel Hood, and took part in an action off Rochefort in which four troopships were captured. (Sir Samuel should not be confused with Admiral Viscount Hood, also named Samuel, who was his cousin. Sir Samuel was one of Nelson's 'Band of Brothers', and like Nelson had lost an arm.)

In 1807 Captain Lukin anchored the *Mars* off Cromer. John Sell Cotman recorded the event for posterity in a water-colour which he called 'The Mars off Cromer'. It can be seen at the Castle Museum, Norwich.

Lukin left the service in 1814, with the rank of vice-admiral. One can say that his service was distinguished, but without any of that greatness that marked out so many of his contemporaries.

In 1824 he inherited the Felbrigg estates and assumed the name of Windham. He set about long held plans to improve and alter the property, but most of these did not come to fruition due to lack of funds. Evidently his share of the prize-money he earned in the *Mars* was insufficient to fund his ambitions in this direction. Perhaps it is as well, for his plans would have produced a different Felbrigg to the well-loved property we can see today.

Admiral Windham died in 1833. He had not been the first, nor was he to be the last man of that name to go to sea. Two of his sons followed him into the navy, and one of his predecessors had sailed as a supernumary on a voyage sent to find the North West Passage. William Windham (1750-1810) had sailed on the voyage to the Arctic in 1773 aboard the *Racehorse*, consort ship of the *Carcass*. One of the midshipmen aboard the *Carcass* had been Horatio Nelson.

There is a portrait of the admiral at Felbrigg. There is also a large painting by Van der Velde in the drawing room there. It depicts 'The Battle of the Texel', of 1673, in which John Narborough took part.

Rear-Admiral Thomas Manby (1769-1834)
Hilgay and Northwold

Captain George William Manby, who became famous for his invention of the first rocket-launched life-saving apparatus, had a younger brother who rose to a much higher rank in the service of his country than did George, who was an artillery officer. (See note at the end of this section.)

Thomas Manby was born at Hilgay in West Norfolk on New Years day 1769. His father had been aide-de-camp to the Marquis of Townshend in Ireland, and used his lordship's influence to get Thomas a post on the frigate *Hyaena*, in 1783. He later saw service on the *Cygnet*, the *Amphion*, and the *Illustrious*.

In 1790, he joined the crew of fellow Norfolk seaman Captain George Vancouver in the *Discovery*, at the start of the great voyage of discovery and exploration to the North West Pacific, 1790-1795.

Manby's abilities must have impressed Vancouver, for in 1793 he was promoted to Master of the consort ship *Chatham*, and subsequently was made 3rd Lieutenant back on the *Discovery*. It is certain that any regard Vancouver may have had for his young officer, was not reciprocated. In a letter Manby called Vancouver, *"Haughty Proud Mean and Insolent."* In another he says, *"Capt. Van(couver) has got quite fat though he has not yet got clear of his Cough. His Language to his Officers is too bad."*

On one surveying expedition on the Pacific coast of North America, two boats were being used. Vancouver was in one, and Manby was in charge of the other. Manby's boat fell behind and then got separated from his captain's. Vancouver was furious over the incident, and Manby was to write, *"... his salutation I can never forget, and his language I will never forgive ..."*. As this incident took place some three months before Manby's first promotion, it is clear that Vancouver himself bore no long term grudge over the matter.

During the voyage, Manby built up a large and enviable collection of native artefacts. The present whereabouts of this collection is unknown, although similar collections made by some of his fellow officers have ended up in the British and Cambridge University Museums.

Vancouver named many of the places he charted after members of his crews. One of the points at the entrance of Yakutat Bay is called Manby Point.

At the end of the voyage, Vancouver was to report to the Admiralty that Manby was, *"active, diligent and deserving"*. Vancouver made an abortive attempt to get Manby's seniority as a lieutenant back dated. This is further evidence of the captain's regard for Manby's abilities.

Whilst in command of the *Charon* from 1797 to 1799, Manby gained a considerable reputation in convoying ships across the Irish Sea, and in operations against French privateers. It is reported that he protected a total of 4,753 ships without suffering a single loss.

At around this time he renewed his acquaintance with one of his *Discovery* shipmates, Thomas Pitt, now Lord Camelford and the sworn enemy of Vancouver. Their friendship was to last until Camelford's death in 1804, and can perhaps be taken as another indication of Manby's antipathy for his old captain.

In 1799 Thomas Manby gained post rank, and was appointed to the *Bordelais*, a captured French frigate. This ship was renowned for its fast sailing capabilities, and for its beauty. She was also thought to be dangerous to sail in, due to the weakness of her frames. In this ship he was instrumental in saving a convoy from a small French fleet.

He later served in West Indian waters. In command of the *Africaine* in 1803, virulent yellow fever broke out on board. Both surgeons died from the disease, and Manby himself acted in their place, and then contracted the fever himself. Over a third of the crew died during the voyage home.

Manby's journal for the *Discovery* voyage contains several references to the appearance of the comely island maidens he saw during that voyage. They give the impression that he was something of a lady's man. This impression is reinforced by the incident which occured about the time he was appointed to the *Africaine*. He had been introduced to the Princess of Wales and it was said that she conducted herself towards him with undue familiarity. The matter caused something of a scandal, and later Manby made an affidavit to the effect that the story was a wicked invention.

In 1808 Manby in the *Thalia* and in charge of a small squadron, cruised the Arctic coast of eastern America. During this period he surveyed and named Port Manvers in Labrador.

This Arctic service on top of his earlier bout of yellow fever finally ruined his health and he had to resign his command. He purchased a small estate at Northwold. In 1810, at the age of 41, he married a Judith Hamond from that village. They had two daughters. The eldest daughter Mary, married first the Baron de Flassons (d.1831) and secondly, Sir Cavendish Stewart Rumbold, Bt. She died at Norwich in 1850.

Thomas Manby was promoted to rear-admiral in 1825. He died from an overdose of opium at Southampton on the 13th June 1834.

Note:

The grave of the more famous of the two brothers, George William Manby, lies close to the south wall of the Church of All Saints, Hilgay. The gravestone is inscribed to 'Captain George William Manby, Royal Navy'. This is incorrect, for George was never in the senior service. He was an artillery officer. How did such an error come about? There are several possibilities.

1. *George was predeceased by both his wives, and by his younger brother. He lived for many years at Yarmouth, and died there in 1854. His body was taken to the other side of the county for burial, and one can assume that there was no one living at Hilgay at that time with a close knowledge of him.*
2. *He was famous for his invention of the life-saving device, and possibly this might have made people assume that his connection with the sea was closer than it in fact was.*
3. *It is said that he attended the Downham Market school at the same time as Nelson. He made this claim himself, although it is perhaps dubious*

in view of their relative ages. He would have only been three when the ten year old Nelson spent his brief period at that School. Nevertheless, Manby played on this connection, and even opened a Nelson Museum at Yarmouth in his later years. This may have caused people to assume that he himself had been a sailor.

4. *Lastly, it is possible that Manby may have had something to do with the inscription himself. Who knows, he might have left instructions to the stonemason. The rank of captain in the navy is, after all, three ranks above that of a naval lieutenant, which is the equivalent rank of a captain in the army.*

Captain John Sanderson (fl.1800-1820)
Captain John Baines (fl.1810)
Kings Lynn

Little is known of the personalities involved in the Lynn whaling trade. This is unfortunate, because the trade was once very important to the town and therefore it, and the people engaged in it, deserve to be better documentated. It flourished in the 17th and 18th centuries, and into the early part of the 19th. At Lynn it was never on the scale of such ports as Hull, Whitby or Dundee, for there were seldom more than three or four whalers based on the port. Nevertheless, small as the fleet was, its activities provided employment not only for the crews involved but for a number of people engaged in the associated shore-side facilities.

The blubber yards at Lynn were situated on both banks of the mouth of the River Nar. Huge copper boilers were used for boiling the whale and seal flesh. The oil produced was stored and distributed in wooden casks, and so there was a substantial cooperage facility close to the yards.

The Lynn whalers operated mainly in the icy waters off the coast of Greenland and especially in the Davis Strait. They sailed out of the port in March, and were back again in August or September. Their return was always an occasion for great rejoicing, not only because they were safely back from a dangerous and arduous voyage, but also because it meant work for many. The first sighting of the ships from the fort was the signal for the bells of St. Margaret's to ring, and this brought people flocking to the river banks.

The information we have on individual crew members is sparse. We know that in the year 1788, Capt. Cook of the Lynn whaler *Archangel* had a dangerous encounter with a polar bear on an ice-flow. He was saved by a lucky shot from the gun of the ship's surgeon. (That small piece of information at least confirms that some of these whalers carried someone with medical training.)

We know a little more about Capt. John Baines of the whaler *Experiment*. A single page of that ship's log survives, and is dated 23rd April 1804, when the ship was off the coast of Greenland. John was the father of Thomas Baines (1822-1875) the artist and African explorer.

Capt. John Sanderson was master of the whaler *Enterprise* which arrived at Lynn in August 1818, with the very large catch of 11 whales. It was estimated that they would produce about 160 barrels of oil which would fetch around £6,000. The whalebone products would fetch a further £18,000. (Whalebone was used for corset and umbrella ribs.)

In 1817, Capt. Sanderson was presented with a silver tea-pot. It was inscribed thus:

To John Sanderson, Captain
of the Enterprise at Lynn
for his services in Greenland
in 1817.

In 1821 Capt. George Manby, the inventor of the rocket life-saving device, made a voyage on the whaler *Baffin*, in order to test a harpoon-gun he had invented. He wrote a journal about this voyage, and it contains a reference to Sanderson:

'. . . we met with the Enterprise of Lynn, Capt. Sanderson. As that officer had interested himself deeply in my invention and had given me much useful information on the whale fishing, I went on board his ship, and requested him to take charge of one of my hand-harpooners, to which he readily acceded, promising to give it the fullest trial whenever the opportunity should offer.' Later on, he refers to Sanderson again, saying that the captain was, *'a gentleman of great ability and possessed of an experience of 20 years in the subject,'* (Manby's harpoon-gun was not a success. From the point of view of whale conservation, that can only be a cause for celebration.)

As gas lighting came to the town of Lynn, the whaling trade died, for the oil was no longer needed for lamps. By the mid-1840's, White's Directory could report that:

'Lynn had formerly 3 or 4 ships employed in the whale fisheries of Greenland and the Davis Strait, but since the demand for oil has been greatly decreased by the introduction of gas, this hazardous, but often lucrative, trade has been here discontinued, though Hull, Whitby and some other places on the eastern coast are still engaged in it to a considerable extent.'

The typical whaler of the late 18th century would have been a three-masted vessel of around 300 tons. The hull would have been specially strengthened for working in the ice, by a sheathing of an extra layer of planking. Additional cross-beams would have been added inside. She would have carried a crew of about 40.

These whalermen were a tough lot. They needed to be, for their work was both hard and dangerous. Even without the dangers of having to navigate in ice, the actual work on the catch was extremely hazardous. It was not unknown for boats to be smashed by one sweep of the whale's tail as they moved in for the kill.

Once the whale was dead, there was the task of towing it back to the ship. All the ship's boats joined in this laborious job, and when the ship was reached, the whale had then to be cut up — the process was called 'flensing' — into convenient sized pieces for storing in the casks provided. This was dirty work, and the smell associated with it was atrocious.

When a whale had been caught, the crew were often rewarded with extra rations, sometimes with grog. (Some whaling ships were known to have been owned or commanded by men with temperance leanings, and on those ships all strong drink would have been banned.)

When one considers how tough these men were, it is perhaps surprising that many of them produced, in their brief time-off periods, items of great beauty which are now considered to be collector's items and are keenly sought after. Their pieces of scrimshaw, carved whale teeth and bone, were often very delicately decorated with whaling scenes, a product very difficult to associate with the hard, horny hands of these shellbacks. They carved a lot of cribbage boards, for that was the favourite game aboard these ships.

Whalermen had their own form of sea-shanties. The last verse of one of them went like this:

'O Greenland is a dreadful place
It's a place that's never green;
Where there's ice and snow and the whale fish blow
And the daylight's seldom seen, brave boys,
And the daylight's seldom seen.

There is a creamware jug in the Castle Museum at Norwich with a verse on it which gives us the names of another Lynn whaling captain and his ship.

A ship from Lynn did sail
And a ship of noble fame
Captain Baxter is the commander
The Balaena is her name

We know that the Balaena (named after the latin for whale) was sailing out of Lynn in the late 18th century.

The demise of this trade at Lynn would have brought sadness and unemployment to many. To some, however, it would have been a blessing. The smell from the boiling blubber vats was supposed to have been powerful enough to spread for miles around and permeated everything it came into contact with.

In these days when conservancy of our ocean wild life is such an important issue, it is perhaps worth noting that it was barely more than half a century ago, that a certain Canadian gentleman was awarded the OBE 'in recognition of his success at the seal fishery'. The man was Captain Abram Kean; the date of the award was 4th June 1934, after he returned from the icefields with his 1,000,000th seal.

Joseph Hume (1777-1855)
Winterton

Joseph Hume was a radical politician of the first half of the 19th century. He was a believer in Free Trade, he protested against the impressment of sailors, flogging in the services, imprisonment for debt, and just about everything else. He became a sort of one man, self-appointed guardian of the Exchequer, keeping a watchful eye on all government expenditure. He was a thorn in the flesh of many ministers and sometimes, apparently, of his constituents. In 1839, as the member for Kilkenny, he was pressed by them to take the Chiltern Hundreds. He refused, stating that he made it a fixed rule on no account to accept any sinecure office.

Hume was born at Montrose, and graduated as an MD in 1796. Soon after that he entered the service of the East India Company as a ship's surgeon.

The ships of the Company at this stage in its development were often some of the best afloat. This did not prevent the crew's quarters in them being crowded, damp, cold, and often dirty. There was little in the way of ventilation. A sick-bay of sufficient size to isolate sick seamen was the exception rather than the rule. Scurvy, typhus and dysentery were common. So was venereal disease. Consumption and pneumonia were also prevalent. In these conditions, and given the state of medical knowledge of the time, a surgeon's life on board was not an enviable one.

By the time Hume went to sea, the position of the ship's surgeon had risen somewhat from the old Barber-Surgeon status, but not by that much. Hume would probably have been in receipt of an allowance towards the cost of his medical chest, but it may not have been sufficient to cover the full cost. A glance at the list of instruments carried will give some idea of the nature of his task:

Amputating knives
Amputating saw with spare blade (!)
Bone nippers and turnscrew
Silver catheters,

are just a few of them.

The surgeon would have been expected to hold daily surgeries, and to keep proper records. He might have an assistant in the form of a surgeon's mate. He was in fact, physician, surgeon and apothecary.

Hume did not stay a ship's surgeon long and, under those conditions, who can blame him. Ashore in India, he made himself an expert in Indian dialects, and became the Company's official interpreter. He must have been extremely diligent and hardworking, for he combined that duty with the offices of paymaster, postmaster, and commissariat officer. He made himself a fortune in the process. He returned home from the sub-continent in 1808 a very rich man.

He purchased Somerton House, (which he renamed Burnley House after his wife's maiden name), near Winterton where he died in 1855. There is a tablet commemorating him in Holy Trinity Church there.

Captain Sir William Hoste (1780-1828)
Godwick

William Hoste went to sea as a protégé of Nelson. In addition to his Norfolk origin he had other things in common with his patron. His father too was a clergyman, and young Hoste also attended the Paston Grammar School at North Walsham.

The Reverend Dixon Hoste, William's father, married Margaret Stanforth of Salthouse. They had six sons and four daughters. The living of Tittleshall was in the gift of the Coke family, and when it was granted to Dixon Hoste he had taken up residence in nearby Godwick Hall.

William was born at Godwick on 26th August 1780. At the age of seven he became a boarder at a school in King's Lynn, before attending the Paston School. Through the good offices of the Cokes, Hoste senior obtained an introduction to Nelson and, in 1793, William joined Nelson in the *Agamemnon.*

The decks of this ship must have resounded with the Norfolk accent. Nelson had recruited many local volunteers, including four who were entered on the books as 'captain's servant'. Hoste was one of these, Nelson's stepson Josiah Nisbet another. The other two were John Weatherhead son of yet another Norfolk clergyman, and William Bolton, who was related to the captain through the marriage of Susannah, Nelson's sister.

Hoste was to see plenty of action during his first years at sea. He was at the battle in which Nelson lost the sight of his eye. He followed Nelson into the *Captain*, and was at the Battle of St. Vincent. Nelson had nothing but praise for the young man. Hoste's feeling for his captain came close to adoration.

He followed Nelson into two other ships, the *Irresistible* and the *Theseus*. In the latter ship, he was at the battle off Tenerife where Nelson lost his right arm. In this action, his friend and by this time Lieutenant, John Weatherhead, was mortally wounded. Hoste was promoted in his place, and wrote, *"happy would it have made me had it been in any other vacancy as I shall ever regret the loss of him".*

In 1798 Hoste presented himself for examination for lieutenant, and his testimonials included one each from Thomas Coke and Lord Townshend. He passed, and continued his service in the *Theseus*, but now under the command of Captain Ralph Milne. This ship took part in the Battle of the Nile, at which Nelson flew his flag in the *Vanguard*. The *Theseus* was the ship immediately ahead of the flagship in the British line. Milne, like many of Nelson's 'band of brothers', must have been something of a glory-hunter. He camouflaged his 74 gun third-rate with painted awnings to make it look from a distance as if it had an extra deck with proportionately more guns! During this battle, Hoste was ordered away to board one of the French vessels, but it was blown up before the boarding could take place.

After this battle Hoste was given his first command, that of a captured brig called the *Mutine*. At Naples in this ship he met Lady Hamilton for the first time. She was quite taken with the young man and said "he will be a second Nelson".

Hoste had his troubles aboard this vessel for it was the common practice of the time to crew such small vessels with the fleet's misfits. Hoste had to order several men flogged.

He was made post-captain in 1802, being given command of the frigate *Greyhound*, and in the following year after ten years away from home, he was ordered back to England. During these years away he had picked up some reasonable sums in prize money, useful additional emoluments for one whose father was rashly extravagant and always in debt.

In 1804 he was given command of the frigate *Eurydice* and again served in the Mediterranean. Involvement in several actions resulted in more prize money.

On October 1st 1805 Hoste dined with Nelson aboard the *Victory*, and on the 13th he was given command of the *Amphion*, one of the navy's best frigates. He was sent on a diplomatic mission to Algiers. There is a possibility that Nelson, who knew that a great action against the old enemy was imminent, deliberately sent his young protégé away from the danger area. If that was the case, then it is doubtful whether Hoste would have appreciated the careful regard of his patron. As it was, he missed the Battle of Trafalgar. When he later heard the news of Nelson's death, he wrote to his father, '*Not to have been in it, is enough to make one mad; but to have lost such a friend besides, is really sufficient to almost overwhelm me.*'

During the next few years, Hoste was almost continually in action in the seas around Italy and Sicily. By this time he had his younger brother Ned on the ship with him as a midshipman. More prize money was earned; in a period of three months during 1808, he took a total of thirty-eight merchant ships.

On 13th March 1811, Captain William Hoste fought the battle which has provided a set piece for several of the modern authors of naval fiction. It is known as the Battle of Lissa. In it, Hoste with four frigates mounting a total of 124 guns, and with 900 men on board, engaged a much larger Franco-Venetian fleet. The enemy had six frigates and five smaller ships, mounting 276 guns, and manned with over 2,000 men.

With the *Amphion*, and under Hoste's overall command, were the *Active, Cerberus*, and the *Volage*. The first sign of the impending battle was at three o'clock in the morning when the *Active*, which was out of sight of the other ships, gave a pre-arranged signal with guns and a blue flare, to indicate that she had sighted the enemy. Two hours later, the ships in the main squadron were able to see the *Active*, and as it got lighter, the masts of the enemy squadron appeared out of the morning mist. Although the French and Venetians had the weather gauge, Hoste did not hesitate. Inspired by the thought of his patron's famous signal before Trafalgar he ordered the signal 'Remember Nelson' to be raised. As this signal was read and repeated, and relayed to the British crews, cheering and waving broke out on each of the four ships. Captain Hornby of the *Volage* wrote of the event, '*Never again so long as I live shall I see so interesting or so glorious a moment*'.

By early afternoon, the battle was over. The French flagship, *La Favorite*, had run ashore and blown up, and three other frigates had been captured. It had been one of the most remarkable small ship actions ever, with victory going to the side which in every respect had been vastly outnumbered.

Captain Sir William Hoste
(National Maritime Museum, London)

When Hoste and his small flotilla returned to Valetta with the captured ships, he was given a hero's welcome. The garrison spontaneously turned out to cheer the ships in. However, although when news of the victory reached England the achievement was appreciated, for some reason Hoste did not get the honours he expected and deserved. Rear-Admiral Charles Boyles, himself a Norfolkman from Wells, had compared Hoste's victory with that 'of our immortal countryman; Lord Nelson'. Even if allowance is made for a certain amount of regional pride in the admiral's statement, there were many who would have agreed with him. Apparently the Admiralty did not. There was not even a knighthood, an honour given many times previously for much lesser achievements.

When later that year Hoste returned home, he was fêted around his native county, but received little in the way of recognition elsewhere. The Admiralty did permit him to have his choice of the new frigates being built. He chose the *Bacchanti*.

He sailed in that ship in 1812 to join the Mediterranean fleet under Sir Edward Pellew. His brother sailed with him again as midshipman. Another Norfolk lad joined them. He was Charles Anson, related to the Coke's by marriage, and a great-nephew of Lord Anson, the circumnavigator. This young man was to die in an unfortunate accident involving one of the ship's guns, and he was buried in the cemetery at Lissa.

By now Hoste was suffering from rheumatic fever and malaria, but these illnesses did not prevent him giving distinguished service in the Adriatic campaign against the French. In January 1814, he captured the towns of Callabra and Ragusa (Dubrovnik) by setting up batteries of guns on hills overlooking these towns, a task that had previously been thought impossible. Later that year, his health deteriorated further, and he was invalided home.

This time, his excellent record was at last rewarded. He was created a baronet and courted Lady Harriet Walpole whom he married in 1817. He saw a little more sea service, but his feeble health ensured that his great days were over.

He was one of the committee set up to raise the money and commission the 'Norfolk Pillar', a 144 foot tall memorial to Nelson erected at Great Yarmouth in 1819, twenty years prior to the more famous one in Trafalgar Square. He actively campaigned against the Impress Service. In 1825 he was appointed to command the royal yacht, a post of high prestige in the peacetime navy.

In 1828 he and his family (he had three sons and three daughters) moved into a house he had bought at Petersham in Surrey. He died there on the 6th December of that same year, of tuberculosis. Like his patron, he had not lived to see 50.

His eldest son, William Legge George Hoste, inherited the baronetcy. He entered the navy and died a rear-admiral in 1868. As the captain of *HMS Spartan*, he arrived in Rajah Brooke's Sarawak on March 28th 1857, with orders to protect British lives during the Chinese insurrection there.

In the market place at Burnham Market there is an inn called the 'Captain Sir William Hoste'. Its bar has as a feature a large mock-up of the bow section of the captain's most famous ship, the *Amphion*.

Captain Frederick Marryat (1792-1848)
Langham

Close to the south-west corner of the Church of St. Andrew and St. Mary, in the quiet and lovely Norfolk village of Langham, lies the grave of probably the best recruiting agent the navy ever had.

Captain Frederick Marryat, with his books on sea life which include 'Mr. Midshipman Easy', 'Frank Mildmay', 'Masterman Ready', and 'Jacob Faithful', has influenced generations of young men to enter the navy, or to take up other maritime careers. Joseph Conrad, perhaps the greatest of all writers about the sea, once said that it was Marryat's writings that inspired him to take up a seafaring life. Although less fashionable now, the books are still read, and they form a body of work probaby unrivalled as a source of information on life in the navy during the first half of the 19th century.

Marryat the novelist has tended to push Marryat the sailor into the background. In fact, he had a particularly distinguished naval career, and had he not annoyed both King and Establishment with his anti-press gang stance, he would probably have reached flag rank.

He was born in London in 1792. He was the second son of Joseph Marryat, a man of some substance, one-time M.P. for Sandwich, a Chairman of Lloyds, and an owner of several plantations in the West Indies. Frederick's mother was the daughter of an American Loyalist.

His school days were characterised by truancies and a lamentable lack of academic diligence. He tried to run away to sea on more than one occasion. When he was fourteen, his father let him have his way, and he joined the *Impérieuse* as a Volunteer 1st Class.

He was lucky in his first ship, for she was commanded by the most famous of all frigate captains, Thomas, Lord Cochrane, 10th Earl of Dundonald. Cochrane's exploits in this ship became the pool of experience on which Marryat based many of his stories. Under Cochrane, the *Impérieuse* and her crew were engaged in a series of battles, cutting-out operations, and what today would be called commando actions. For a young man looking for adventure spiced with danger, his three years under Cochrane could scarcely have been bettered. Cochrane liked him, and he was always in the thick of things. He was wounded three times, once even being left for dead.

It was aboard the *Impérieuse* that the most extraordinary aspect of Marryat's sea career began. He jumped overboard to save the life of a fellow midshipman at Malta, and this was but the first in a long series of such events. A reading of his biography leaves one with the impression that he spent almost as much time in the water as on it! During his career he received no less than 27 recommendations for saving lives at the risk of his own. On three occasions, he jumped overboard at sea in attempts to save lives, and on at least one of these, was miles astern of the vessel before being picked up. In 1818, he was awarded the Royal Humane Society's gold medal. The citation read, *'For the saving of at least a dozen lives at the imminent hazard of his own'*.

Captain Frederick Marryat
(National Maritime Museum, London)

After leaving Cochrane's ship, he saw service on the *Centaur*, the *Atlas* and the *Africa*, before joining the *Aeolus* under Captain Lord James Townshend in 1811. He probably saved the lives of the entire crew of this ship, when he voluntarily led the gang which cut away the mast and rigging as she lay over on her beam ends in a roaring gale. Lord Townshend thought so anyway, and wrote a commendation to that effect.

In 1812 Marryat was examined for the rank of lieutenant, passed and was promoted. Around 1815, he invented the first widely used Code of Signals, which later became the basis of the first International Code. (In 1833, in recognition of this work, he was made an Officer of the Legion of Honour by Louis Philippe of France.) In 1819, he was made a Fellow of the Royal Society, and he married his wife Catherine in that same year. She presented him with four sons and seven daughters, but not all of them survived into adulthood.

He was given his first command in 1820, of a ship called the *Beaver*. This ship was stationed at St. Helena to guard the exiled Napoleon. Marryat was there when the Emperor died, and made a sketch of the body. Prints made from an engraving of his drawing were once very popular in France.

In the *Rosario* in 1821 he had a brief period with the preventive service in the Channel. This gave him material for his book, 'The Three Cutters'.

Later in the 1820's he took an important part in the Burmese War, and in consequence was appointed a Companion of the Bath. He left the navy in 1830, having already had two of his books published. In that same year he purchased an estate of 1000 acres at Langham, and took up farming.

He became the proprietor and editor of the Metropolitan Magazine, and many of his stories were serialized in it. In all, he wrote 22 books, including several for children. His 'Children of the New Forest' is still popular. He developed a wide circle of literary friends. It included Dickens, Landseer, Lytton, George Cruikshank, and Ainsworth.

His farming ventures were not successful. The records show that in most years his farm expenditure exceeded the revenue earned. He became interested in a project for draining some salt marshes at Cley-next-the-Sea, but it didn't come to anything.

He was on friendly terms with the Townshends of Raynham Hall. He wrote, *'That polka is certainly an epidemic. I was at Raynham ... and the Townshends were dancing it there and gave me a lesson'*. It was likely to have been during one of his visits that he first heard of the ghost of Raynham. (The ghost, known as the 'Brown Lady', is supposed to be that of Dorothy Walpole, sister to Sir Robert, Prime Minister.) Marryat, the macho seaman, scoffed at the story, so was invited to stay at the Hall to meet her himself. He was given a room where a portrait of the lady herself was hung. This enabled the captain to recognize her when he and two friends saw her walking along a corridor. The men hid in a small room, but the 'Brown Lady' stopped outside the door and smiled at them. Marryat fired a pistol shot at her, and the ball was said to have passed through her, without making her lose her grin. We are not told whether or not the captain maintained his disbelief in ghosts after that. In fact, we are left with the niggardly doubt that perhaps, in view of the gun he carried, his original disbelief may not have been too firm.

Marryat took up permanent residence at Langham in 1842. He became a magistrate and Deputy Lieutenant for the County. His last years were troubled with illness and not a little eccentricity. He had sixteen chiming clocks installed in his house, and went to great lengths to ensure that they all struck at precisely the same moment.

For one who had saved so many from a watery grave, he was to experience a tragic and ironic twist of fate. In December 1847 he received the news that *HMS Avenger* had been lost when she hit a reef in the Mediterranean, and that most of the crew had drowned. Among the missing was his son, Lieutenant Frederick Marryat.

Captain Marryat did not get over this blow. He died a very sad man, just before dawn on the 8th August 1848. It has been said of him that, 'he was never content with one place or one mode of life for long'. Perhaps if he had been content to stay at sea, and perhaps if he had not written his novels, he might have been ranked among that vast host of sea officers whose names, if they are remembered at all, are known only to the naval historian. His novels, however, have assured him of a place in any history of English literature.

The model for Mr. Midshipman Easy, may have been Thomas Robert Keppel, younger brother of Admiral of the Fleet Sir Henry Keppel. Thomas sailed under Marryat on the West Indian station, but didn't like the life, and took up the ministry instead. He eventually became the rector of North Creake. The villagers there are convinced that their one-time parish priest was the prototype Easy.

Commander Samuel Harmer (c.1793-1843) Great Yarmouth

The long Norfolk coastline with its sandy dunes alternating with long stretches of marshland, has always been a boon to those engaged in smuggling. The many havens and inlets made the landing of smuggled goods easy, and the inland waters of the Broads with their associated rivers facilitated onward distribution.

One of the favourite haunts of smugglers was the 'White Horse Inn' at Gorleston, and another was the 'Wherrymen's Arms' on Sutton Broad. The former has been pulled down, but the latter is now part of the 'Sutton Staithe Hotel'. The wherries were the ideal medium for distributing smuggled brandy and geneva, which came into Yarmouth or Gorleston on fishing boats, and Sutton, lying at the head of the Broads system, made a perfect depot.

Throughout the 18th century, and until 1831 when the responsibility for the coastguard service was given to the Admiralty, the preventive service, including the coastguard, was administered by the Board of Customs. Until 1788, many of the revenue cutters were owned and operated by contractors, who were recompensed by taking a share of the profits made by the sale of seized goods; an inefficient system, open to abuse.

After the naval battles of the Napoleonic Wars were over, many of these cutters were commanded by naval lieutenants on half-pay. There had never been any love lost between the navy and the preventive service. Each was envious of the others rights and authority, especially where joint operations against smuggling were involved. There was always contention over the rights of search — it was not unknown for naval captains to be engaged in smuggling — and over prize-money. It would not be overstating the situation to say that the navy despised the customs service. So it must have been something of a humiliation for some of the naval officers concerned to find that their only opportunity for sea-going employment was aboard coastguard cutters.

These cutters were built for speed. They usually had one mast, with an enormous sail area for their size. To facilitate the carrying of the giant-sized jib-sails, which augmented the large gaff-mainsail, the vessels were fitted with bowsprits almost as long as their hulls. There was a law against the fitting of these bowsprits on any other craft, in order to tip the balance of any chase towards the government side. The cutters usually carried a crew of about 30, and were fitted with up to 14 guns. One such ship, the *Hunter*, was lost with all hands off Happisburgh in 1807.

Samuel Harmer, a native of Great Yarmouth, spent most of his service career as a coastguard officer. He was the son of a merchant, and passed his lieutenant's examination in 1814. We know little of his exploits against smugglers, apart from the fact that he commanded the cutter *Royal Charlotte* for part of the time.

Harmer took part in several notable rescue operations. In one, he saved the lives of two men from the *Westmoreland*, and was presented with the silver medal of the Suffolk Humane Society. In another, in 1823, he helped with a rescue which used Captain Manby's rocket apparatus (first used successfully at Yarmouth in 1808).

He advised on improvements to the buoyancy of local lifeboats, a fact that was noted by the Suffolk Humane Society.

In 1830 he was made Chief Officer of the Coastguard at Yarmouth. He must have been pleased when in the following year, that service came under the jurisdiction of the Admiralty. He was promoted to commander in 1837, and in 1840, after a quarter of a century's service on the East Anglian coast, he was given command of the steam vessel *HMS Driver*, and sent to the China Station. He died out there in 1843.

There is a memorial to Samuel Harmer on the north wall of St. Nicholas Church, Yarmouth, and the Maritime Museum of East Anglia has a portrait of him. He is often wrongly called 'Captain' Harmer. In the Navy Lists of his time, his name disappears after 1843, and then he still held the rank of commander. It was the custom at one time for naval officers, upon retirement, to adopt the next rank up from their substantive rank. This would not have applied in his case, as he died 'in harness'.

The Reverend Richard Johnson (fl.1788-1827)
Ingham

Partly upon the recommendation of one-time mariner Pastor John Newton, Richard Johnson was appointed Chaplain to the First Fleet in 1788. This was the fleet which carried the first convicts to Botany Bay. After the ships arrived there, he was made Chaplain to the colony, and in that position was fourth in the pecking order of responsibility, ranking next after Governor Phillip, the Lieutenant Governor, and the Judge Advocate.

Johnson stayed there for twelve years, returning to England in 1800. From 1813 until 1827 he was Vicar of Ingham in the County of Norfolk.

By the time Johnson was appointed Fleet Chaplain, the position of minister aboard naval vessels had become one of some status. This had not always been the case. Chaplains were not carried as a matter of course, and in earlier times even when they were carried, their social position on board was often at the whim of the captain. Their pay was often on par with that of an ordinary seaman. In the early 17th century, things improved somewhat, when it was decreed that a deduction was to be made out of seamen's wages, and the resulting sum became the chaplain's stipend. Thus his emoluments depended upon the size of the crew. There was sometimes doubt as to whether all or, indeed, any of this money found its way into the pocket of the chaplain, but at least it was an attempt to regularize his position on board. Chaplains were not paid a fixed salary until 1812.

Unlike naval surgeons, who started in much the same position, and who eventually gained commissioned status with a progressive ranking system, chaplains have always maintained their semi-civilian status although they now wear uniforms.

When, in 1790, the Second Fleet arrived in Australia (the land was not officially called that until after Matthew Flinder's voyage of 1801-1803), Johnson recorded some facts about the condition of the convicts on board. They do not make pleasant reading. Out of 499 convicts who embarked on the *Neptune*, for example, 158 had died at sea, and another 269 arrived in a very poor state of health. The chaplain said that he could not face going below decks on that ship, as the smell and infestation were so bad. He stated that one man had 10,000 lice on his body. One wonders how he counted them.

Rev. Johnson survived the appalling conditions of the first two years of the Botany Bay Colony. Everyone there, officials, soldiers, and convicts, came close to starvation during that period, as the promised store-ship did not arrive. This ship was the *Guardian*, and the reason for its non-arrival will serve to illustrate the dangers involved in one of the methods used at that time to replenish the fresh water supplies on board.

In 1789 Captain Edward Riou (who had been a shipmate of Vancouver under Capt. Cook, and who was to die an heroic death at the Battle of Copenhagen) was given command of the sloop *Guardian*. It left England with stores, passengers, and convicts, for the new colony. It called at the Cape for extra stores and cattle. On Christmas Eve, in the icy seas of the South Indian Ocean, whilst attempting to take on ice to replenish the ship's water supply, the ship struck a submerged part of an iceberg. She was badly holed, and water began coming in fast. Then she lost her rudder, and on Christmas Day when all hope had gone, Riou ordered the boats launched. There was not enough room in them to carry all on board, so the captain and about sixty men stayed behind.

Captain Riou sent a farewell note with one of the men in the boats, and when finally this man was picked up by a French merchantman, it was assumed that Riou and the rest of his men had perished. However, two months later, after he had managed to extricate his ship and after a very hazardous and difficult voyage, he managed to get her back to the Cape. She was in such bad condition on arrival that she was beached there, and the infant colony at Botany Bay did not get its stores that year.

Captain Riou's achievement has few parallels as an example of skilful seamanship. It is of interest to note that one of the men who stayed with him on the damaged *Guardian* was Midshipman Thomas Pitt. This young man somehow blotted his copybook, for seven years later Riou refused to sign Pitt's letter of recommendation for promotion to lieutenant. This same Thomas Pitt, later Lord Camelford, was the gentleman Vancouver was to order flogged, and who was to make a misery of that navigator's last years.

Richard Johnson spent those first lean years in the colony, ministering to the spiritual needs of his flock. To him fell the privilege of conducting the first Christian service in Australia, on the 3rd February 1788. His task could not have been an easy one for, quite apart from the unusual make-up of the group from which his congregations came, he was not helped by the rather indifferent attitude of Governor Phillip. In 1789, Johnson supervised the opening of the first school at Sydney.

After he arrived back in England, as well as holding the living at Ingham, Richard Johnson was rector of a city parish in London. The church concerned no longer stands, and his memorial tablet was moved to St. Mary Aldermary Church in London.

Rajah James Brooke of Sarawak (1803-1868)
Norwich

James Brooke gains his place here because he attended Norwich Grammar School as a pupil.

He was born in 1803 at Benares in India, where his father was a judge in the service of the East India Company. At the age of 12 he came home and became a boarder at the school in Norwich. He didn't like it there much, but then most boys are not over fond of their schools. He ran away from it, after his best friend there had left to go to sea. An application was later made for him to be re-admitted, but the school was having none of it. In later years, when he had become a legend in his own lifetime, the school was happy to proclaim that he had been one of their most gifted students!

At the age of 16 he returned to India as an army ensign, rose to be a lieutenant, was wounded in battle, and finally invalided home in 1825.

In the years 1830-1831, in a ship named the *Castle Huntley*, he visited Penang, Malacca, Singapore and China. In 1834 he bought the brig *Findlay*, loaded it with trade goods, and once more sailed for the east. The venture was a failure, and he sold both ship and cargo at Canton at a loss. In the following year he bought the armed schooner *Royalist* with money left to him by his father. After what would nowadays be termed a 'shake-down' cruise to the Mediterranean, Brooke set about teaching himself navigation, and he read everything he could find on the East Indies. He had come under the spell of that magical corner of the world, a spell that has continued to lure many Englishmen over the intervening years.

He sailed for the Far East in late 1838, with a crew of nineteen. When he arrived at Singapore he was commissioned by the Governor and the Chamber of Commerce to convey to the Rajah of Sarawak gifts and letters of thanks for the good treatment he had recently afforded to some shipwrecked English seamen. On the voyage across the South China Sea, Brooke carried out some survey work to correct some of the information on the rather poor charts of the area that were then available.

His reception at Kuching, the capital of Sarawak, was a good one, and very soon his fascination for the east became focused on this small part of the island of Borneo. Over the next few years, in between trading voyages to Singapore, he helped quell a rebellion and fought several sea and land battles with local pirates. In 1841 he was made acting Rajah by the Sultan of Brunei, overlord of most of the north-western coast of the island. A year later Brooke was confirmed in the post of Rajah. No Englishman (apart from his two successors) has ever held a similar position in a foreign land.

In his continuing battle with pirates and insurrectionists, Brooke now received help from the British government in the person of the Hon. Capt. Henry Keppel aboard his ship *H.M.S. Dido*. Brooke and Keppel became fast friends, a friendship that was to last until Brooke's death. When the *Dido* left to join the fleet in Chinese waters, her place was taken by *H.M.S. Samarang*. One of the midshipmen on board that ship was another man with Norfolk connections, Frank Marryat (youngest son of the novelist) who wrote an interesting account of his adventures in *H.M.S. Samarang* whilst it was in Sarawak waters. Apparently he liked the Dyak maidens, for he wrote of them, *"Their eyes are dark and piercing, and I may say there was something wicked in their furtive glances. Their hair was superlatively beautiful, jet black, and of the finest texture, hanging in graceful masses down the back and nearly touching the ground".*

Over the next few years James Brooke consolidated his position and extended his domains. He was aided on many more occasions by the navy, and by ships of the East India Company. All the parties concerned were anxious to eliminate piracy in the area. Keppel and the *Dido* returned, and aboard this time was a nephew of Brooke's, Midshipman Charles Brooke. He was to become the second White Rajah.

James Brooke was now famous. He returned to England in 1847, and although he had his detractors, he was fêted everywhere. He took great pleasure in the romantic image that had built up around him and his achievements. He was knighted by the Queen, and Oxford made him an honorary Doctor of Laws.

When he returned to Sarawak, piracy had once again become rife. Another campaign was launched against it, and this time was conducted with so much violence that it received harsh criticism from a number of quarters back in England. One of the critics was Joseph Hume M.P., by now a resident in Norfolk. He called Brooke 'a mad despot', and argued that the Rajah should be made to refrain from 'further massacres'.

At about this time, Brooke caught fever and very nearly died. This was followed by a bout of smallpox, and when he finally got over that, the handsome hero of the Sarawak legend had disappeared for ever. His face was disfigured and his hair had turned white. The illnesses had, however, taken away more than his good looks. He became indrawn and markedly less active.

In 1857 the Rajah had to cope with a serious uprising of the Chinese living in Sarawak. Several Britons were murdered during this revolt, and it was put down by a force of Malays and Sea Dyaks led by Brooke and his nephew (who had by now left the navy). Although they attempted to restrain the practice, they were not successful in preventing their Dyaks from returning from these forays with strings of shrunken heads.

During this uprising the navy sent a ship to Sarawak to protect British lives. The ship was the *Spartan*, and she was commanded by Captain Sir William Hoste, Bart., the son of the hero of Lissa.

From that time on, everything was downhill for James Brooke. He was in England from 1858 until 1860. He was in his mid-fifties, but looked twenty years older. He was having problems with the British Government over the future of his little eastern kingdom. He was also having problems over which of his kinsmen was to succeed him. He never married, but did have an illegitimate son, possibly by an English maidservant.

He returned to Sarawak twice during his last years to sort out problems there. In 1863 he left his kingdom for the last time. Although he kept a distant finger on the pulse of far-off Sarawak, he left the government of his state in the capable hands of Charles.

James Brooke died in June 1868, at his Devon home. He was buried in Sheepstor Churchyard. The church there has a commemorative window to him.

Admiral of the Fleet Sir Henry Keppel (1809-1904) Quidenham

Henry Keppel had a maritime forbear of no inconsiderable quality, for he was the grand-nephew of Augustus, Viscount Keppel (1725-1786) who became First Lord of the Admiralty, and who as a young man had sailed around the world on Anson's famous voyage.

Henry was born at Kensington in 1809, but spent much of his childhood on the family estates at Quidenham, Norfolk. He was a sickly youth, after having been an even sicklier baby. The story goes that as a young child it was once considered that he had died. He was saved from burial only by the vigilance of the family nurse.

He entered the navy at the age of 13, and at the Cape nearly died of fever on his first ship. After passing his examination he was promoted to lieutenant in 1829. As a young officer it appears that he might have been a bit of a rebel. It is on record that he jeopardised his career while serving in the West Indies, by *'breaking an arrest in order to attend a charity ball'*. In 1832 he was involved in a duel at Trincomalee. He had the reputation of being both truculent and pugnacious; perhaps that was his way of compensating for his small stature, for he was only a little over 5 feet in height. Many years later, Queen Alexandra was to call him her 'beloved little admiral'.

He saw active service in support of the forces of the East India Company. He was promoted to commander in 1833 and, in command of a small brig, took part in actions against the Carlists on the south coast of Spain.

He was promoted to captain in 1837. Two years later he married his first wife, Katherine, the daughter of General Sir John Crosbie: she died in 1859. Later, when in command of the corvette *Dido*, he served with some distinction on the China station and, in 1842 as senior naval officer at Singapore, he met James Brooke for the first time. Keppel set about the task of aiding the White Rajah in any way he could against the Borneo pirates. In 1844, with the *Dido* and the East Indiaman *Phlegethon* and some of the Rajah's forces, he attacked a large pirate settlement. The fighting was bitter and lasted for four days. Keppel was later to write of the encounter, *'Headless trunks, as well as heads without bodies, were lying about in all directions; parties were engaged hand to hand, spearing and krissing* (the kris is the native Malay dagger) *each other'*. Thirty-two British seamen were killed in the battle, and another thirty injured. The enemy losses were estimated at ten times as many, and they lost over 200 boats.

Keppel then returned home and spent two years on half-pay, before being given command of the frigate *Maeander* in 1847. In this ship he returned to Sarawak and renewed his contacts with Brooke. Like his friend, he had developed a love and fascination for that part of the world, and the local Dyaks had honoured him with the title 'Rajah Laut', or Sea King. He returned to England via Australia and the Magellan Strait. On that commission he lost over half his men from battle and disease.

In 1853 he was given command of what was considered to be one of the finest ships-of-the-line in the navy, the *St. Jean d'Acre*, and in her took part in the Baltic campaign. In the Crimean War, he commanded the Naval Brigade at the siege of Sevastopol. For his work here, he received several honours including that of Companion of the Bath.

Next he commissioned the frigate *Raleigh*. His officers included a prince, a couple of lords, and a scion of the Montagu family. This assemblage of the aristocracy did not prevent the ship from hitting an uncharted rock off Hong Kong, however. The ship was lost, but all the crew were saved. Now a commodore, he was given a chartered steam vessel called *Hong Kong*, and brilliantly led an action against the Chinese in the Canton River. On the recommendation of his admiral, he was knighted for these services, and afterwards promoted to rear-admiral.

His subsequent career is a story of promotions, senior commands, and court appointments. He married again in 1861 — to Jane West, who bore him a son and daughter. For a period he was commander-in-chief at the Cape, and served in the same capacity on the China station a few years later. He was liked and admired by several members of the Royal family, and enjoyed a close relationship with some of them.

He was made an admiral of the fleet in 1877, and remained on the active list until he died — an unusual honour. He died in 1904 at the venerable age of 95, quietly in his bed. He was buried at Winkfield. There is a memorial to him in Quidenham Church.

The Chinese called the harbour at Singapore, Lung-Ya-Men, or Dragon Teeth Gate. Col. William Farquhar, the 1st British Resident there, changed its name to the rather prosaic New Harbour in 1820. On the 19th April 1900, it was renamed again. They called it Keppel Harbour after Sir Henry. The stretch of water leading to the harbour had been called Keppel Roads since 1885.

There have been one or two attempts made to compare Keppel's service with that of Nelson, and to put him on par with the hero of Trafalgar. Such a comparison is not sustainable. Keppel had many of the Nelsonian qualities, but he was born fifty years too late. His active service was spent mainly fighting pirates and insurgents, and he was involved in no great sea battles.

Captain Samuel Gurney Cresswell (1827-1867) King's Lynn

In the year 1845, Sir John Franklin sailed for the Arctic with the *Erebus* and the *Terror* to look for the North West Passage. He disappeared forever. At some time during 1847 or 1848, it has been surmised, the Passage may have been discovered by some of his sledge parties, but there is no definite proof, as no member of his expedition lived to tell about it.

Several expeditions were sent out to look for Franklin. Then in 1850, two ships, the *Enterprise* under Captain Richard Collinson, and the *Investigator* under Commander Robert McClure, left England for the Alaskan coast via the Horn. Their orders were to search for the western end of the Passage and to look for traces of the Franklin expedition. Lieutenant Samuel Cresswell of King's Lynn was aboard the *Investigator.*

The ships parted company during the voyage out, and the *Investigator* arrived off the Alaskan coast first and commenced the search. In October, McClure, Cresswell, two other officers and six seamen, made a land excursion on Victoria Island. They fought their way up a 1400 foot mountain through deep snow. When they reached the summit, they had a clear view of a field of sea-ice, which they knew could only be the Melville Sound. As this sound had earlier been reached by Parry from the opposite direction, the party knew that the North West Passage, that had eluded the searches of sailors for centuries, had been discovered. (It was left to Captain Francis McClintock in the *Fox* expedition of 1857-1859 eventually to find many relics of the Franklin expedition, including his last message. In addition, the Passage was not to be traversed in its entirety until Amundsen sailed through it in 1905/1906.)

The *Investigator* and its crew spent many more months exploring the area. In 1853 Cresswell was put in charge of a group on a mission to get a sick seamen to the depot ship *North Star.* There he joined a returning supply ship for the voyage home to England, which was reached in October of that year. Only then did the world learn of the discovery that had been made nearly three years previously, and it was a Norfolkman who had brought home the news.

Samuel Cresswell gained his captaincy in 1858. He died on August 14th 1867.

Over the years many men and ships had been lost looking for the Passage. Yet when it was finally discovered, it was found to be of little commercial significance. It was not used commercially in fact, until 1969, when it was traversed by the tanker *Manhattan.*

Admiral of the Fleet Lord Fisher (1841-1920) Kilverstone

John Fisher fought in no major battles, and therefore is unlike most of the other admirals with Norfolk connections mentioned in this book. He did not have many opportunities to distinguish himself in battles of any kind, yet he has left his mark on the navy in a way that had scarcely been equaled previously, and certainly has not been since his death. It was he that dragged the old navy of Nelson, whether it liked it or not (and very often it was the latter) into the 20th century.

He was a man you either adored or hated. He was not physically attractive, yet it seems that he fascinated most of the women he came into contact with, including Queen Victoria. He made many powerful friends, and many equally powerful enemies. He was not a discreet man. The preface of one of his books contains the lines:

"Sworn to no Party — Of no Sect am I!
I can't be silent and I will not lie!"

So he knew exactly what he was like! So did Winston Churchill who once said of Fisher that he was, *'amazingly voluminous and reckless in correspondence'*. Coming as it did from a man who himself was not known for pulling his written punches, or his verbal ones for that matter, that statement is illuminating. Fisher's indiscretions too, were not just confined to the written word; his utterances were often loaded with derogatory remarks about persons and institutions he did not agree with. He hated inefficiency in any form, and when he saw it, no matter if tradition or custom stood in his way, he had no hesitation in stomping all over it.

When he reached high command and other senior naval officers objected to the changes he was pushing through, his reaction was to say, 'Sack the lot!' That became one of his favourite sayings. He said of war, that in it, *'You have to be ruthless, relentless, and remorseless'*. He also said that it was, *'rot to talk about civilised warfare, you might as well talk about a heavenly hell!'* It was almost as if he foresaw the way that the 1st and 2nd World Wars were to be fought and, however one might disagree with his philosophy, it was he who was largely responsible for the fact that the British Navy was in good shape at the start of the first of those wars.

John Arbuthnot Fisher was born at Rambodde, Ceylon, on 25th January 1841. His father, a soldier, was ADC to the Governor of that colony. At the age of six, John was sent home to England and lived with his grandmother. He did not have a happy childhood.

In 1854 at the age of thirteen he entered the navy as a midshipman. He joined what was then a depot ship, the *Victory* at Portsmouth. Appropriately in view of the ship he joined, the man who used his influence to get Fisher into the navy was Admiral Sir William Parker, the last living member of Nelson's band of captains.

Unlike a lot of officers of that time, John had to live on his service pay. He had no private income. This meant that he had to eat the food officially provided, and his writings confirm that the food on board Her Majesty's vessels had not improved much over the years.

He saw his first sea service in the *Calcutta*, which conveyed troops, stores and munitions, to the Baltic fleet during the Russian War. In 1856, on the *Highflyer*, he went to the Far East. He must have conducted himself well out there, for he came to the notice of the commander-in-chief and was transferred to the flagship, and subsequently promoted to acting lieutenant. He returned home in the *Furious* in 1861. The captain of that vessel wrote him a testimonial that said, *'as a sailor, an officer, a navigator, and a gentleman, I cannot praise him too highly'*.

Fisher won the coveted Beaufort Testimonial — a prize for the best navigation paper — in the examination for lieutenant. He was appointed gunnery officer of *HMS Warrior*, the first ironclad battleship built for the navy (and the last to survive, for she has recently been conserved). He married Frances Broughton in that same year, and they were to have one son and three daughters. All the daughters eventually married naval officers.

He spent two periods at the *Excellent*, the navy's gunnery school, and during the second of those started the torpedo school there.

At the age of thirty-three he was promoted captain. Already he had the reputation of a man who liked change, a man almost a visionary, in marked contrast to most of his fellow officers who liked and were satisfied with the old and outdated navy of Nelson.

After some more sea service in the Mediterranean and North Atlantic stations, he was recalled to oversee the fitting out of the revolutionary *Inflexible*, a battleship of 12,000 tons with the heaviest armour and guns of any ship afloat. She was full of new inventions, and was the first ship in the navy to be fitted with electric lighting. In 1882, this ship under Fisher took part in the bombardment of Alexandria, and he distinguished himself in charge of the Naval Brigade there.

He was made a Commander of the Bath, and from then on, was to get an annual invitation to visit the Queen at Osborne.

He collaborated in the authorship of a publication that criticised the then state of the navy, and this helped to bring about improvements. In 1886 he became the Director of Naval Ordnance, and in 1890 was made rear-admiral. Later, as admiral-superintendent at Portsmouth Dockyard, he was able to get the battleship *Royal Sovereign* completed in record time. He was knighted in 1894, and promoted to vice-admiral two years later.

As commander-in-chief of the North American and West Indian station in 1897, he had the job of welcoming a visiting American fleet under the command of an admiral who can best be described as being sparing of speech. After a lengthy speech of welcome from the British side, the American admiral replied with what Fisher later said was the best speech he had ever heard. The American said, *'It was a damned fine old hen that hatched the American Eagle!'*, and promptly sat down.

Two years later as C-in-C of the British Mediterranean fleet, the world's largest, he set about improving it. He made many administrative changes. He

Sir John Fisher
(National Maritime Museum, London)

improved strategy, conducted regular exercises, raised training methods, and brought in economy measures. He made many new enemies in the process.

In 1901, he was made a full admiral, and a year later became 2nd Sea Lord. In this position his views and innovations met with more hostility, but that did not stop him from pushing most of them through. He set up the Royal Naval College at Osborne, and then turned his attention to that class of craft which came to be called 'Fisher's toys', the submarine. He may well have been the first to appreciate the importance of these craft, and of their future effect on naval warfare. In a famous memorandum in June 1913 he said *'(The Submarine) cannot capture the merchant ship; she has no spare hands to put a prize crew on board ... There is nothing else the submarine can do except sink her capture ... it is freely acknowledged to be an altogether barbarous method of warfare ... (but) the essence of war is violence, and moderation in war is imbecility.'* Winston Churchill, then First Lord of the Admiralty, told Fisher, *'I do not believe this would ever be done by a civilised power'.* We were to find out very soon that Fisher's sombre predictions about modern total warfare were indeed accurate.

He was made 1st Sea Lord in 1904, and was to stay in that post for five years. Once more he rode roughshod over his opponents. Any officer who did not agree with him was sacked and put on half-pay. He brooked no argument, unless it was constructive — from his point of view. His list of enemies became longer.

At the stroke of a pen he got rid of about a hundred old ships by scrapping them, or selling them, or by relegating them to the reserve. 'Sack the lot!', became 'Scrap the lot!' However, the ships that were placed in the reserve were made ready for instant mobilisation by giving them 'nucleus' crews, instead of 'skeleton' crews. He reorganised the dockyards, and selected Scapa Flow as a suitable base for the Home Fleet.

He placed the order for *HMS Dreadnought*, a battleship of 18,000 tons, mounted with ten 12 inch guns, and with a speed of 22 knots. When launched, she was the most powerful warship afloat. He introduced the class of battle-cruiser. In the teeth of violent opposition, he began the process of substituting oil for coal as the navy's fuel.

By a special Order in Council in 1906, he was made an admiral of the fleet. In 1909 he was raised to the peerage, taking the title of Baron of Kilverstone in the County of Norfolk. His coat of arms and his motto are of interest. Instead of the more usual animal supporters to his arms, his are supported by two British tars. (In heraldic vernacular, *'on either side a sailor of the Royal Navy supports in the exterior hand an anchor cabled, that to the dexter in band sinister, and that to the sinister in band dexter, all proper'.*) His chosen motto was, *'Fear God and Dread Nought'.*

His quarrels with certain members of the naval establishment, and his draconian methods of pushing his ideas through, finally put him in the position of having to resign, which he did in 1910.

But the naval scene had not seen the last of Lord Fisher. After the forced retirement of Prince Louis of Battenberg in 1914, and at the age of seventy four,

Fisher was recalled to the post of 1st Sea Lord. It was his foresight in despatching two battle-cruisers, the *Invincible* and *Inflexible* from the Grand Fleet in home waters, that resulted in the British victory at the Battle of the Falklands in 1914.

When German Zeppelins started bombing Britain, he put forward the proposition that for every civilian killed in these raids, one German internee should be executed. Perhaps he was not putting this forward seriously, but anyway, fortunately it was not taken up.

He opposed Churchill (who was 1st Lord of the Admiralty) over the Dardanelles venture, and resigned in 1915, mainly because of this.

He died in his bed on 10th July 1920. One suspects that he would have preferred a more heroic death, perhaps like that of his hero Nelson. Looking back with the advantage of hindsight, it may not be overstating it to say that his contribution to the well-being of his country and to the navy, was equal in value if different in composition, to that of Nelson.

Lord Fisher thought, by the way, that Nelson had been poorly done by his country, both in the matter of the title Nelson was awarded after the Battle of the Nile ('a Common or Garden Lord', says Fisher) and in the way Emma Hamilton was treated after the great man's death. He says of the latter, *'She died in penury and found a pauper's grave in a foreign land. A passing Englishman paid her funeral expenses. It makes one rise up and say "Damn"!'* Most of us would agree with him.

Unlike many of his peers, Admiral Fisher had a great regard for the Merchant Navy. He called it, *'the magnificent Merchant Navy of the British Nation'.* He said of the merchant ship losses of the Great War, *'Seven million tons sank under these men, and the record of so many I've seen who were saved was: "Three times torpedoed". And remember! for them no Peerage or Westminster Abbey. They didn't even get paid for the clothes they lost . . . '.* Later he said that a flame should be lit for, *'the great Merchant Navy that saved our country!'* One knows just how Fisher would have reacted towards those responsible for the present parlous state of the Merchant Navy. 'Sack the lot!', he would have said.

Lord Fisher was given a public naval funeral in London, but there was to be no Westminster Abbey for him either. At his own request, he was buried in the quiet Norfolk countryside in Kilverstone churchyard.

For him no vulgar celebration,
Donated by a grateful nation;
Just a simple graveyard plot,
For the man who sacked the lot,
During the task of preparation,
Which made victory, the culmination.

Captain Richard Woodget (1847-1928)
Lt. Commander Edgar (Jack) Woodget (b.1905)
Burnham Norton
Burnham Overy Staithe

The *Cutty Sark* is arguably the most famous of all clipper ships. There can be no argument that the most famous of her captains was Richard Woodget.

Woodget was born at Burnham Norton in 1847, not very far away from Nelson's birthplace at Burnham Thorpe (Nelson's father was rector of both places in the mid-18th century). After he retired from the sea, Woodget lived in nearby Burnham Overy Staithe. His house, called Flagstaff House, still stands just across the road from a marshy inlet. Woodget's eighty-two year old grandson Jack, a retired Lt. Commander RN., still lives in that village, and has a fund of stories to tell about 'the old man'.

Captain Woodget joined the *Cutty Sark* in 1885, and was to stay with her for ten years. During that period both ship and shipmaster were to become legends. At a period when it was becoming difficult for any sailing ship to pay her way (this applied especially to a small one like the *Cutty Sark*) Woodget regularly made the voyage out to Australia in seventy days, and back in eighty. He drove his ship and his crews hard. About half of his ship's complement always consisted of young boys, as an economy measure. Some of them were only thirteen years old.

Woodget was a consummate seaman and a fine navigator. He was an exceedingly tough disciplinarian, given — as were most of his breed — to hard fighting and hard swearing. His young men had a hard life but they learned their trade well. Men who had spent part of their training under him usually had no difficulty in obtaining employment in their later careers, and many of them rose to the top of their profession. (Several, including Captain C. E. Irving, CB, RD, RNR., became commodores of the P. & O. Line). As training under Woodget was something of an accolade, it was once said that it seemed an inordinate number of aspiring officers had claimed to have served with him. Grandson Jack has the answer. He says that his grandfather was so tough, that one voyage under him was enough for most young men!

Many stories have been told about the *Cutty Sark's* career under Woodget in the Australian wool trade. Perhaps the most famous is the one about the encounter with the P. & O. liner *Britannia*. This steamer was making for Sydney Harbour Heads, and passed the *Cutty Sark* in a near calm heading for the same destination. Woodget signalled a request that the *Britannia* report the *Cutty Sark's* forthcoming arrival. The wind got up during the night, and when the steamship sailed through the Heads the following morning, there was the *Cutty Sark* at anchor in the harbour. *'For all the world looking as if she had been there for a week'*, the *Britannia's* master was later to report.

Woodget had two hobbies, and two rather unusual pastimes. He indulged in them all aboard his ship, and he was very good at them. He bred collie dogs

of high quality. His favourite was one called Lassie, and when she died at sea he had her stuffed. She ended up just inside the door of Flagstaff House, and Woodget would never pass her without patting her on the head. 'For good luck', says Jack.

His second hobby was photography, and one of his photographs is famous. It is the one taken of the *Cutty Sark* under full sail in mid-ocean. Woodget took this with his camera tripod standing on a plank lashed across the gunwales of two side-by-side life-boats let out on the end of a long hawser from the ship. The boats were manned by Woodget himself and 'volunteer' apprentices.

His pastimes, which he insisted his apprentices take part in, were roller-skating and cycling. The 'tween decks were used as a rink when the ship was in ballast. One imagines that both pastimes were dangerous in anything other than a dead calm. The cycle used was one of the old bone-shakers.

Woodget had four sons; Richard, Harold, Edgar and Sydney. The first three followed their father to sea, and spent some time in the *Cutty Sark*. Richard rose to be mate of the ship, and ended up as a captain in the Blue Funnel Line. The other two also achieved command rank.

When he retired, Captain Woodget bought a small farm at Burnham. As with everything else he turned his hand to, he was good at it. It was very profitable. He kept pigs, chickens, and rabbits, and also ran a hackney pony stud. It was the realisation of many a retired sailor's dream.

Throughout his life, Woodget had a habit of chewing on one side of his moustache whenever he was angry or excited. Apparently one half of his hirsute appendage used to disappear completely inside his mouth on such occasions. It did this one day when Woodget and his grandson took one of the ponies along to be shoed. The pony was skittish, and the blacksmith struck out at it with his hammer. The hard-case ex-mariner hit the blacksmith in the mouth, causing the loss of six teeth and a subsequent court case.

'The old man was tough right up to the end', says Jack Woodget. *'He was very hard with me when I helped him on the farm, and one day we had the most terrible argument. The upshot of it was, that I went along to the nearest naval recruiting establishment (at Brancaster) and joined the navy. I knew that would annoy him no end, as he had the most extraordinary antipathy towards the navy!'*

In 1924 at the grand age of 77, Captain Woodget took command of the *Cutty Sark* once more, when she was moved to take part in a regatta. For many years of his retirement he was the local collector for the Shipwrecked Fishermen and Mariners' Royal Benevolent Society. When he died on March 5th 1928, it was that institution that subscribed for the stone anchor that lies atop his grave. He was buried in the graveyard of St. Margaret's Church at Burnham Norton.

On the front of Flagstaff House at Burnham Overy, there is a plaque stating that the captain once lived there. It is not an official one. It was put there by one of the subsequent owners of the house. The man with the proper sense of history, was 'Uncle Mac' McCullock who for so long compèred the BBC Radio programme 'Children's Hour'.

Jack Woodget was born in 1905, and joined the navy in 1921. He specialised in gunnery, eventually becoming a commissioned gunner.

He served in some famous ships. These included the *Barham*, the *Iron Duke*, the *Revenge*, and the *King George V*. He says modestly, that he saw little of the war. *'I was always tucked away in a well armoured gun-control tower.'* However, when he was serving in the *Iron Duke* at Scapa Flow, he witnessed the loss of the *Royal Oak*. He was awarded the MBE in 1953, and retired from the navy in 1955. From 1956 until 1979, he was Clerk to the Council at Overy Staithe.

The *Cutty Sark*, built for Captain John Willis in 1869, now lies preserved in her Greenwich drydock. The memory of her tough, no-nonsense, and most famous captain, is preserved in the mind of his grandson. Jack is a bright-eyed, still active, and forthright, octogenarian. One suspects that Jack is a chip off the old block, and that he takes no inconsiderable pride in being just that. And why should he not?

Coxswain Henry Blogg GC, BEM. (1876-1954) Cromer

The weather off the east coast of England on 13th December 1933, was very nasty indeed. There was a gale blowing from the east, and it was bitterly cold. The seas were running unusually high.

Up and down the east coast it turned out to be a busy day for the lifeboats. They could do nothing however, to save nine men on the *Culmore* off Aldeburgh, and another ship, the *Broomfleet*, was lost with all hands.

The maroons first went up at Cromer at about 4 a.m. A barge called the *Glenway* had gone ashore off Happisburgh. The Cromer lifeboat *H.F.Bailey* under the charge of Henry Blogg, was launched and fought its way down the coast. When they reached the barge, they found that she was ashore in shallow waters, and with seas breaking all round her it was impossible for the boat to get close. For two hours they stayed in attendance, waiting for the tide to ebb enough for the men on board the barge to be able to reach the shore by their own efforts.

As his crew were by now wet, tired, and very cold, Blogg decided to run with the weather south to Gorleston rather than to try to get back to Cromer. He was not to know that at about the time he made that decision, a similar stranding was happening off Cromer to the north.

The barge *Sepoy* with two men aboard had anchored off there to ride out the gale. As the storm worsened, the anchors dragged, and the sea pushed the craft remorselessly towards the beach under the eyes of an ever-growing crowd of onlookers.

Heroic attempts were made to launch the Cromer second boat with a scratch crew aboard. On the third attempt they were successful, and the lifeboat was manoeuvred close enough to the *Sepoy* to get a line on board. Then the sea took charge again, the line parted, and the lifeboat was swept over the breakwater and up on to the beach.

In the meantime efforts had been made to contact the *Bailey*. The Gorleston lifeboat was launched, and they managed to rendezvous with the *Bailey* some eight miles north, and passed the message across about the *Sepoy*. Blogg did not hesitate. He turned his craft around and headed north. He was later to say that the journey up and down the coast on that December day was the worst in his experience. Other east coast lifeboatmen were later to confirm that the sea conditions were as bad as they had ever seen.

Nearly four hours later, four hours of continuous battling against the sea, the *Bailey* was sighted from the cliffs at Cromer. By then the *Sepoy* was aground about 200 yards from the shore with her deck awash. She was beginning to break up as the seas pounded at her.

Three times Blogg attempted to get his lifeboat alongside the wreck on its shore side. On the third try a line was got aboard, but this carried away as the seas sent the *Bailey* crashing against the side of the barge. She was swept clear, but was holed in the process.

Blogg then decided on a course of action unparalleled in lifeboat history.

From the shore side he drove the *Bailey* right on to the deck of the barge. The lifeboatmen managed to grab the mate just before their boat was sucked off and swept clear. With one man still left clinging to the wreck, Blogg decided to try the manoeuvre again. With consummate seamanship, he again drove his craft up on to the deck, and the second man was taken off before the sea once more swept the lifeboat clear. The *Bailey* had been badly damaged, but the men had been saved.

For his services on that day, Henry Blogg was awarded a second clasp to his Silver Medal, by the Royal National Lifeboat Institution.

Blogg was born on February 6th 1876 in a cottage which is now the 'Wellington Inn' in New Street, Cromer. At school he was considered to be a good scholar, but he was to leave when he was only 11½ to join his stepfather's crab boat as a crew member. The boatmanship he learnt in that trade was to serve him in good stead in his career with the lifeboats. He was to be a life-long teetotaller and non-smoker and, extraordinarily, he never learnt to swim.

At the age of 18, in 1894, he became a member of the lifeboat crew, and took part in his first rescue in the winter of that year. In 1909, he was made coxswain, a position he was to hold until he retired in 1947. During his service with the lifeboats he helped save nearly nine hundred lives.

He was involved in many epic rescues. In 1927, when the Dutch tanker *Georgia* went aground on the Haisborough Sands, he saved fifteen men. In 1938, when the Spanish *Cantabrian* was shelled outside British territorial waters by one of Franco's ships, he saved eleven. The *Mount Ida* struck the Ower Bank in 1939. He saved twenty-nine Greek seamen from that one.

He won the Lifeboat Institution's Gold Medal (an award often and correctly compared with the Victoria Cross) three times and their Silver Medal four times. He was awarded the George Cross and the British Empire Medal. Throughout his life he hardly ever left the county and, on the few occasions that he did, it was usually to pick up one or other of his awards.

Late in his life, and like Captain Marryat before him, the sea from which he had saved so many lives was to bring him personal tragedy. In the summer of 1953 his two nephews were drowned when their fishing vessel capsized off Cromer beach.

Henry Blogg died on the 13th June 1954. He was buried in the 'new' cemetery off Holt Road, Cromer.

There are at least a dozen churches along the Norfolk coastline which contain plaques and boards which list the lives saved by the local boats. They pay stark testimony to the courage of the men engaged in this, one of the most humane of callings.

Lieut. Colonel Alfred E. Knights, DSO, MC, MM, TD (1893-1971) Great Yarmouth

Colonel Alfred Knights was in command of the 4th Battalion of the Norfolk Regiment at the fall of Singapore in 1942. He was later senior British Officer at several of the prisoner-of-war camps on the notorious Burma railway. One of these was the camp built to house the prisoners involved in building the bridge across the River Kwai. Pierre Boulle's book, 'The Bridge on the River Kwai', is a work of fiction, but some of the best characteristics of that author's 'Colonel' are reflected in the considerable character of Alfred Knights.

During those months of imprisonment on the banks of that river, one wonders how often the colonel allowed his thoughts to follow the course of it down to the sea. Did he ponder on the fact that had he not been colour blind, his career would have taken a different direction and he would have probably avoided the horrors of working on that infamous railway? How ever often these thoughts came, one thing is certain, he never let them interfere with his steadiness of purpose, his fortitude and courage, as he strived to better the lot of his men.

Knights had started his working life as an indentured apprentice aboard sailing vessels. He was born in Wellesley Road, Great Yarmouth, in 1893, where his father was a draper. In February 1909, he signed Apprentice's Indentures with the Liverpool shipowner Charles de Wolfe & Company. With this document he bound himself to work for that company for a period of four years. In return, he was to be paid the total sum of thirty pounds spread over that period. It was not a princely sum, but then the salaries paid to cadets and apprentices in the merchant navy, never have been. (In 1946, a cadet with a British tramp ship owner could expect a wage of £2-10-0d a month during his first year of service.)

Knights' first ship was the four-masted, iron-hulled barque *Matterhorn*. His first voyage was around the Horn to Portland, Oregon, and it was to be a trip he remembered for the rest of his life. There were nine other apprentices on board, and they formed about a third of the crew. This large complement of apprentices was one way shipowners had of reducing their overall crew costs.

Apprentices were usually given the hardest and dirtiest tasks to do. However, young Knights was no whinger — his small 5ft 4inch frame must have been extremely tough. The voyage out to Portland took 147 days, and in a letter sent to his sister from that port, he wrote, "... *I can work like a horse. Am as healthy as I can be. Can eat enought to satisfy 3 men but still do not get enough. Climb like a monkey and hang on to a yard by the skin of my teeth and, well there's not much but what if any one else can do it, I can. I cannot help thinking of the rough time we got around the horn. There were chests, boots, clothes, soap, books, blankets all having a waltz in the water in the half deck ... If we got three hours sleep in a night we thought ourselves lucky. Tell Uncle Billy that if he wishes I had chosen something else, I don't. I am quite satisfied except for grub*". Already the youngster was exhibiting signs of the resilient character that was to stand him in such good stead, some thirty odd years into the future.

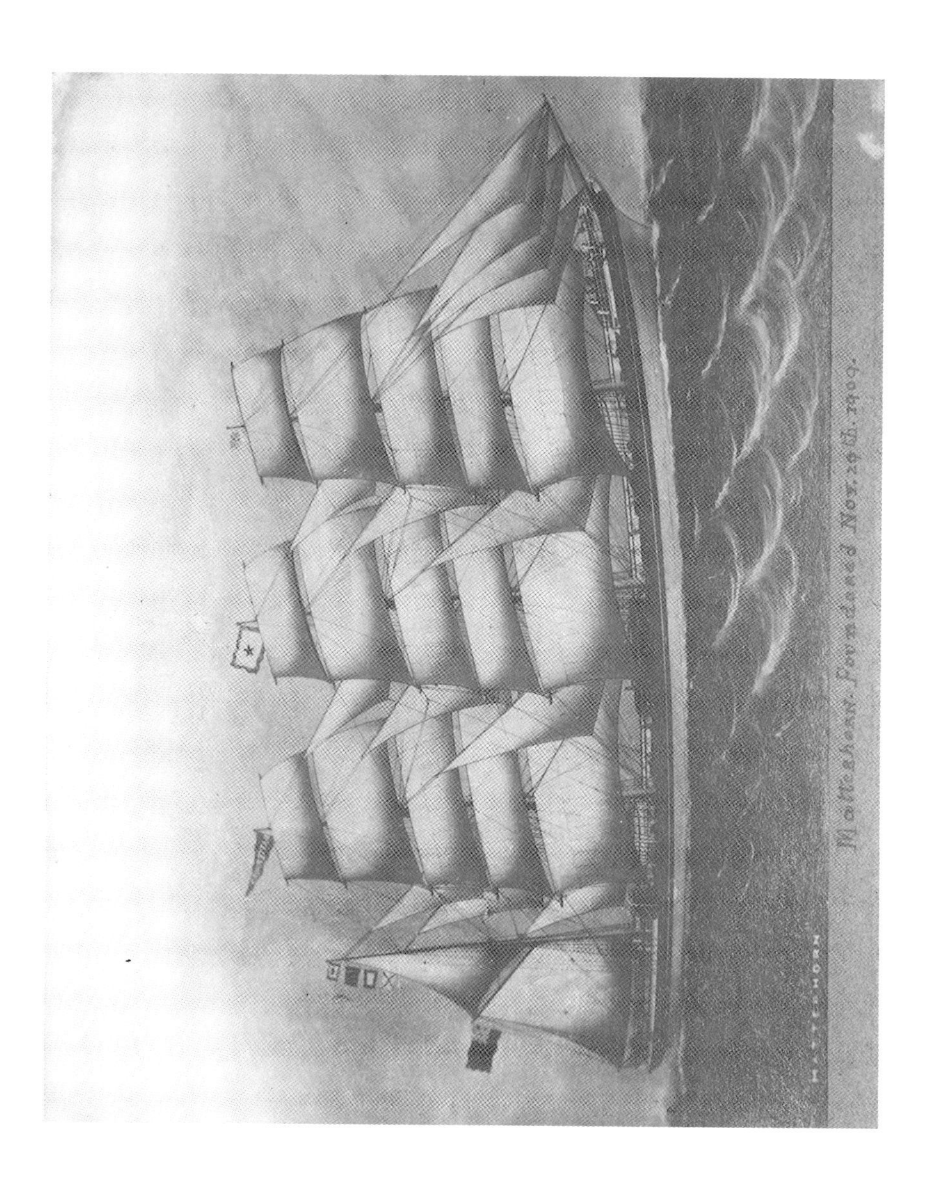
MATTERHORN
Matterhorn. Foundered Nov. 29th. 1909.

The *Matterhorn* loaded barley in bags at Portland for Ipswich, England. A good part of the crew deserted there, a common enough occurence in those days after a hard voyage. Often these desertions were aided and abetted by the local 'crimps'. Crimps were men, and often women, engaged in the practice of luring men off one ship, with promises of women and drink, and then selling the services of the seamen involved to the next ship that came in. Sailors often woke up with sore heads, aboard a ship far worse in reputation than the one they arrived in port on.

Replacements were found for the missing crewmen of the *Matterhorn*, even though both captain and mate were hard cases, according to Knights.

After loading, the ship proceeded down river with the aid of a tug. Captain Salter decided to anchor off Astoria at the mouth of the Columbia River until a strong westerly gale had decreased. Both anchors dragged however, and the captain decided to beat offshore. The ship had developed a list to starboard — grain cargoes, including those stowed in bags, were notoriously prone to shifting. Throughout the night, as the ship attempted to clear what was a lee shore, the list became worse. Heavy seas breaking over the deck prevented the removal of hatch covers to examine the cargo. Suddenly, the steering gear carried away, the ship turned into the wind, and in a matter of minutes her sails had blown to shreds. Several hatches were stove in, and all hands were set to the pumps.

Huge waves now smashed the deck houses, and washed overboard three of the four boats the ship carried. The ship leaned over farther until she was almost on her beam ends. The crew began to jettison cargo, but by the early hours of the following morning it became obvious that the ship could not be saved.

The only boat left could not be launched in the normal way, for it was on the port, now the high side. Waiting for a suitable moment, and as the ship lurched farther over to starboard, the captain gave the order to cut the boat's lashings. As it slid across the deck and into the sea, the crew followed it.

Knights was nearly drowned, but was finally plucked from the water by others who had reached the boat first. The captain, who had a bad head wound, and 26 others were packed into the boat. Three others, including the mate, were lost.

Twenty-seven hours later, the survivors managed to reach the Umatilla Reef lightship. They had to be lifted on board, they were in so bad a condition.

Most young men might have thought twice about staying at sea after such an experience. Alfred Knights was not made like that. He sailed in several other Cape Horners over the next four years. He must have been bitterly disappointed when, in 1913, he tried to sit for his second mate's examination, only to find he was debarred because he was colour blind. Then, as now, that effectively put a stop to any sea career.

Knights started to train as an engineer with the Yarmouth Generating Station, but in 1914 he enlisted in the Norfolk Regiment, and was sent to France. He was wounded and awarded the Military Medal in 1916. He was then commissioned and won the Military Cross. He ended the war with the rank of captain.

He returned to the electricity industry, and over the next twenty years, held various senior positions at Yarmouth, Southport, and Bury-St-Edmunds. He kept his contact with the Norfolk Regiment as a member of the Territorial Battalion.

In September 1941 he became the Commanding Officer of the 4th Battalion, and sailed for Bombay in the *Andes*, and eventually to Singapore on the *USS Wakefield*. For his services in the fighting there he was awarded the DSO but, along with most of his men, he then became a POW.

His notes on his years as a prisoner are voluminous. In them, he vividly describes the horrendous conditions he and his men had to endure. He was impressed with the Australian prisoners under his command. He said of them, *"Their rugged temperament undoubtedly helped them to stand up to the awful conditions and treatment associated with life on the railway"*.

Colonel Knights used many stratagems to help ease the lot of his men. Many stories have been told about them. Perhaps the best known of these occured when the Japanese ordered that all the walking sick were to be placed in working parties the following morning. Knights sneaked 250 of the strongest men into the hospital during the night. They pretended to be ill, and the following morning it was they who were selected to work, leaving the really sick men in the hospital.

After the war ended, Knights returned to the Electricity Industry once more. He even had three years as General Manager of the power authority in Jamaica, after his retirement in this country.

In 1964 he visited Australia in the liner *Southern Cross*, with conditions on board a far cry from anything else he had ever experienced at sea. There he renewed friendships with many of the men he had served with on the death railway.

Alfred Knights died in 1971. His epitaph should read "a very gallant sailor and soldier".

Bertram Nightingale, BEM (1909-1981)
Swanton Morley

Since the earliest times the navy has needed bases, depots and yards around the British coast, in which to lay-up, to careen, to repair, and from which to supply stores to the fleet. Until the end of the 17th century, naval ships only spent winters at sea when it was absolutely necessary, and the off-season months were spent in overhauling the ships. (In the process the crews were paid off with a consequent saving in the wages bill.)

As Britain's interests expanded, a system of overseas bases was created, and at the height of the navy's power this system was world-wide. Major ones existed at various periods at, for example, Simonstown, South Africa, at Hong Kong, at Singapore, at Port Royal, Jamaica, and at Trincomalee, Ceylon (which has one of the finest natural harbours in the world). Wherever the navy needed to be in force, then somewhere near at hand there was a base.

A good example of a home base was at Deptford. The navy had a facility there from the end of the 15th century. In 1742, it became the headquarters of the navy victualling branch, and it enjoyed that position for 200 years. As part of this depot, it had two large rum warehouses; as we shall see, rum was an important factor in naval victualling until quite recently.

As the demand for new facilities was created by an ever growing fleet, they were supplied, although sometimes not so quickly as the navy would have liked. In the 1830's, the old Weevil Yard at Gosport was modernised and renamed the Royal Clarence Victualling Yard — which may sound more grand, but lacks the wonderful evocativeness of the former designation. A rum mixing plant and a cooperage facility for the barrels existed there right up to the end of the naval rum issue in 1970.

As these bases developed, the necessary support personnel were recruited and trained. Various branches of these support services were formed, including those for victualling and ordnance. The various branches had staff members stationed wherever there were bases, and some of them sailed on naval supply vessels.

Bertram Nightingale was such a man. He was born at Gillingham in Kent in 1909, not very far from the Chatham naval base where he started his career as a young man in the victualling branch. (Gillingham was also the birthplace of an Elizabethan who at one time served on a storeship supplying Drake's ships during the fight against the Armada in 1588. He was Will Adams, who has been called 'the first Englishman in Japan', and who was to become, in this century, the model for James Clavell's hero in 'Shogun'.)

After his initial service at Chatham, Bert served at Deptford and at Dover. He spent most of World War II in New York — he got there on the troopship *Queen Mary* — and was awarded his British Empire Medal for his part in setting up the supply organisation there.

After the war he served overseas again, at Trincomalee, at Singapore (twice), and at Hong Kong. Between overseas postings he was stationed at several home depots. His career is a good example of those of that vast band of civilian personnel, often disparagingly referred to by the sea-going community as 'dockyard squadies', but without whom the navy could not have operated efficiently.

Throughout his career with the navy, Bert Nightingale was concerned either in the production of rum, or in the distribution process of getting it to the fleet. This heady concoction had played a very important role in the navy from the 17th century capture by the British of the island of Jamaica. Prior to that, brandy had been the principal soporific on board.

Life on board ships in the period from the 17th to the 19th century was hard. The regular issue of vast quantities of rum, and the not so regular opportunity of earning some prize money, were the things that leavened life on board their majesty's ships, especially for those victims of the press who didn't want to be there in the first place. Over the years, the act of dispensing the daily allowances of rum became a ritual and the high point of a sailor's day. It developed a language of its own, and some of the words and phrases used have passed over into normal English usage.

Rum was issued, subject to the exigencies of battle of course, at precise times every day. At first it was issued neat, at the rate of one pint for a man, and half-a-pint for a boy. In 1740, Admiral Vernon, known throughout the fleet as 'Old Grog' from his habit of always wearing a coat made from grogram, decided that he could not have his men falling about half-drunk all over the place, so he introduced a watered down version. It became known as grog.

At various times over the years, changes were made to the rum issue regulations. Rations were cut, senior ratings were allowed it neat, etc. After a time, one thing did not change however, and that was the formula by which the stuff was made.

It was produced by the navy itself — it was so important that they obviously thought they couldn't trust a contractor to do it properly — to a formula that became standardized. It was a mixture of specific proportions of base rums from various parts of the West Indies, and these proportions were only varied in the direst emergency. "One tried not to mess around with the sailor's staple diet", Bertram once said. The resulting mixture in its undiluted state had almost the consistency of syrup, was nearly black in colour, had a smell that permeated anything that came near it, and at about 120 degrees proof, had the kick of a mule. The sailors loved it. Their other name for it (one of the deepest respect) was Nelson's Blood, called that under the misconception that the admiral's body was returned to England after Trafalgar, pickled in a barrel of it. On special occasions, an extra rum issue was made. This was termed 'splicing the main brace'.

Over the years of his service with the navy, Bert Nightingale came into contact with rum, at the production stage, at the supply stage, and on his own admission, as often as possible at the consumption stage. The saddest day of his entire career was the 31st July 1970, the day when the navy rum issue officially ended. The Admiralty said that it did not fit in with the image of a modern electronic navy. Bert decided that he didn't either. He retired in that same year.

He died at Swanton Morley, Norfolk, in 1981, and is buried in the churchyard there.

Leading Stoker Richard Morris, RN (b.1908) North Elmham

Throughout 1942 the islands of Malta were under siege. Food, fuel, and ammunition were running short. Several attempts were made to get convoys through to the beleagured islands, with great loss of both merchant ships and escorts. Then, in August, the Admiralty organised another convoy, this time made up of 14 merchant vessels, escorted by 2 battleships, 3 aircraft carriers, 7 cruisers, and 24 destroyers. It was the largest ever Mediterranean convoy operation. It was also to become one of the most heroic naval operations of the Second World War.

Having seen the convoy well on its way from Gibraltar, most of the capital ships returned to base, and then the attacks began.

First the carrier *Eagle* was lost. Then the cruiser *Nigeria* was so badly damaged it had to return to Gibraltar. The cruiser *Cairo* was sunk, and the most important of the merchant ships, the tanker *Ohio* carrying much needed aviation spirit, was damaged. The air attacks had by now caused the convoy to be scattered over a wide area and, although valiant attempts were made to round them up, when Italian torpedo boats struck, they found many easy targets. In less than three hours the cruiser *Manchester* had gone down, along with four merchantmen. Later, the *Ohio* was damaged again.

One by one, the surviving merchant ships struggled into the Grand Harbour of Malta, harassed by German bombers every inch of the way. Three disabled merchantmen were still at sea with all the remaining escort ships. One of the three was the *Ohio*. The German bombers struck again, and sank one of the freighters, but one other managed to crawl into harbour.

Of the merchant ships, only the *Ohio* now remained at sea, and she was so badly damaged that she was in the tow of a minesweeper and a destroyer. Bombers attacked again, and the tow rope parted and had to be replaced, but slowly the tanker was nearing the relative protection of Grand Harbour. Getting her there had now become a point of honour, for her crew and the escort vessels. The destroyer *HMS Penn* was lashed alongside the stricken ship, and used her motive power to push them both towards the harbour entrance.

When the ships finally passed between the harbour breakwaters they were given a reception by the waiting ships and crowds that was rarely equalled throughout that war. The master of the *Ohio*, Captain D. W. Mason, was awarded the George Cross. Leading Stoker Morris aboard the *Penn* was awarded £9-10-0d in salvage money!

Richard Morris was born in Portsea in 1908. At the age of 11, he was sent to the Watts Naval Training School at North Elmham, run by the Dr. Barnardo's organisation. He was to stay there for nearly five years before entering the navy in 1924.

The old County School at North Elmham was purchased by Mr. E. H. Watts, of London shipowners, Watts, Watts and Company, in 1902. He made it over to the National Incorporated Waifs Association — Dr. Barnardo's — for the training of boys for the sea services. It could house around 300 boys and, over the years until it closed in 1949, this school set in the heart of rural Norfolk sent thousands of boys into the navies and merchant fleets of Britain, Canada and Australia. (It must be pointed out here that there was no coercion on the boys to go to sea at the end of their training. Most did so, but some did not. This needs to be recorded because this author recently met a lady who was planning to write a book on the 'cannon-fodder' — her expression, not this author's — produced by this school and others like it. Mr. Morris does not consider that he was ever treated as if he were such material, and this author, who attended a similar school, agrees with him.)

Life at Watts, as in other nautical training schools, was hard but not harsh. The food, although never very good, was adequate in quality (as with most young boys, they could have always done with more). One was taught to swim the hard way, by being thrown in, but always under supervision. Come sun or snow, every day one had to swim the length of the open-air and unheated swimming pool. Saturday afternoon was compulsory sports afternoon, but as Saturday morning was compulsory senna-pods morning, it was seldom that any eleven-boy team could be seen on the field at any one time.

(This is a good place to introduce an anecdote from the author's own experience. At his naval school, as an economy measure, no toilet paper was kept in the loos. When one needed some, one had to find the Master-at-Arms and ask for it. This procedure was, of course, sometimes inconvenient! On receipt of such a request this man used to bring forth a sheaf of the stuff from his pocket, always it seemed, with an agonising lack of urgency. He then wetted his fingers, peeled off three sheets which he handed to you one at a time, interposed with the never-to-be-forgotten words, "One up . . . one down . . . and a polisher!")

Richard Morris looks back upon his years at Watts' Training School with affection, so it could not have been too bad. After leaving North Elmham, he did further training at the *Ganges* shore establishment in Suffolk. He then joined his first ship, the carrier *Eagle*. This was followed by service on the Irish Fishery Protection Patrol, before he joined the cruiser *Devonshire*.

In that ship he served in Far Eastern waters. For part of that commission the ship was used to protect British interests at Amoy during the troubles there in the early thirties. He returned home in 1934, made straight for North Elmham, and married a local girl. In so doing, he became the only Watts schoolboy to return permanently — subject, of course, to his sea service — to the village.

During World War II, Richard saw a good deal of active service apart from the *Ohio* convoy. He was on coastal convoy escort duty on the *Wolfhound* in 1940, when she struck a mine and split in two. One half went down, and the other stayed afloat. Richard was aboard the half that sank, but fortunately every one was rescued. (The floating half of the ship eventually made port. Subsequently, it was welded on to the reverse half of another destroyer, and so sailed again.)

Richard Morris left the navy in 1948, one of that innumerable band of unsung heroes who have served their country's navy so faithfully down the years.

The main building of the Watts Training School is no longer there. It has been demolished. Its chapel still stands, although it is now a private house. There is a tiny and beautifully kept cemetery near the site of the school. It contains the graves of sixteen of the Barnardo's boys; sixteen who did not make it down to the sea.

Leading Seaman John H. Pask (b.1930) North Elmham

With the exception of a period in the Korean War, John Pask's career in the navy was a typical peacetime one. It consisted of periods spent 'on station' in various parts of the world, periods on patrol and times spent showing the flag.

John was born in Reepham, Norfolk, in 1930. He entered the navy via the *Ganges* in 1946, at the age of 15½. His first ship was *HMS London*, and on this ship in 1949 he just missed the famous *Amethyst* incident on the Yangtze River, by being sent home on compassionate leave. The *London* was damaged in the incident.

On *HMS Birmingham* in 1952/1953, he took part in the Korean War when the ship was part of the UN Task Force. The ship was mainly engaged in the bombardment of shore positions in support of landing parties. On one occasion the cruiser came into contact with a mine which scraped all along the side of the ship without exploding. When they cleared it, it took only one well-aimed rifle shot to set it off.

On *HMS Defender* in the mid-1950's, John was aboard the ship when it escorted HM the Queen on her state visit to Sweden.

As an example of the geographical diversity of peace-time naval operations, John crossed the Arctic Circle in the *Lagos* during the Cod War of 1958, and was given the usual certificate to commemorate the event. In the following year he got another such certificate for crossing the equator.

John has another interesting certificate. It states that during the seventeen month commission of the *Defender* between June 1955 and November 1956, the ship's company of 318 men, consumed a total of 75,242 tots of rum. As he left the navy in 1960, he did not experience that black day in 1970 when the rum issue was stopped.

John entered the building industry when he came ashore. One of his first jobs was to help demolish the Watts Naval Training School at North Elmham.

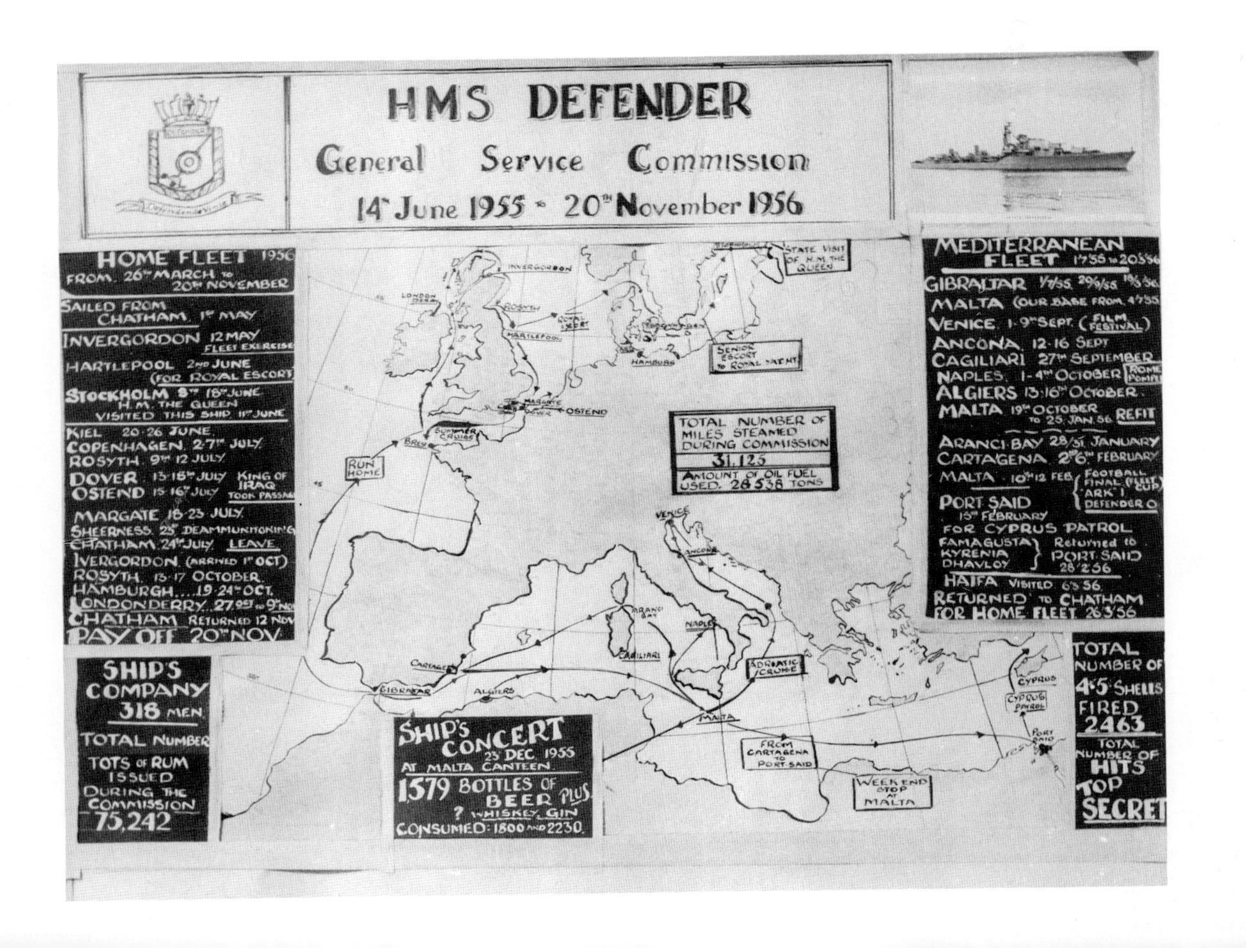
HMS DEFENDER
General Service Commission
14th June 1955 - 20th November 1956
HOME FLEET 1956
FROM 26th MARCH to 20th NOVEMBER
SAILED FROM CHATHAM 1st MAY
INVERGORDON 12 MAY FLEET EXERCISE
HARTLEPOOL 2nd JUNE (FOR ROYAL ESCORT)
STOCKHOLM 8th 18th JUNE
H.M. THE QUEEN VISITED THIS SHIP 11th JUNE
KIEL 20-26 JUNE
COPENHAGEN 2-7th JULY
ROSYTH 9th 12 JULY
DOVER 13-15th JULY
OSTEND 15-16th JULY
KING OF IRAQ
MARGATE 18-23 JULY
SHEERNESS 25th DEAMMUNITIONING
CHATHAM 24th JULY LEAVE
INVERGORDON (ARRIVED 1st OCT)
ROSYTH 13-17 OCTOBER
HAMBURGH 19-24th OCT
LONDONDERRY
CHATHAM RETURNED 12 NOV
PAY OFF 20th NOV
SHIP'S COMPANY 318 MEN
TOTAL NUMBER TOTS OF RUM ISSUED DURING THE COMMISSION 75,242
SHIP'S CONCERT 23 DEC 1955 AT MALTA CANTEEN
1579 BOTTLES OF BEER PLUS ? WHISKEY, GIN
CONSUMED: 1800 AND 2230
TOTAL NUMBER OF MILES STEAMED DURING COMMISSION 31,125
AMOUNT OF OIL FUEL USED 28 538 TONS
STATE VISIT OF H.M. THE QUEEN
SENIOR ESCORT TO ROYAL YACHT
RUN HOME
SUMMER CRUISE
ADRIATIC CRUISE
FROM CARTAGENA TO PORT SAID
WEEKEND STOP AT MALTA
CYPRUS PATROL
INVERGORDON
ROSYTH
HARTLEPOOL
HAMBURG
OSTEND
MARGATE
VENICE
ANCONA
NAPLES
CAGILIARI
ARANCI BAY
CARTAGENA
GIBRALTAR
ALGIERS
MALTA
CYPRUS
PORT SAID
MEDITERRANEAN FLEET
GIBRALTAR
MALTA (OUR BASE FROM
VENICE 1-9th SEPT (FILM FESTIVAL)
ANCONA 12-16 SEPT
CAGILIARI 27th SEPTEMBER
NAPLES 1-4th OCTOBER
ALGIERS 13-16th OCTOBER
MALTA 19th OCTOBER to 25 JAN 56 REFIT
ARANCI BAY 28/31 JANUARY
CARTAGENA 2nd 6th FEBRUARY
MALTA 10th 12 FEB
PORT SAID 15th FEBRUARY FOR CYPRUS PATROL
FAMAGUSTA KYRENIA DHAVLOY
Returned to PORT SAID 28.2.56
HAIFA VISITED 6.3.56
RETURNED TO CHATHAM FOR HOME FLEET 26.3.56
TOTAL NUMBER OF 4.5 SHELLS FIRED 2463
TOTAL NUMBER OF HITS TOP SECRET